S U S A N
WATSON

FOREWORD

You're able to read — or throw aside — this collection of columns because of the work and dedication of a number of co-workers who pushed me and prodded me until this task was done. Editors Marty Hair, Michele Vernon-Chesley, Alice George and Kelly Feusse, whom we lovingly call Old Bud, made my words sound the way I've always wanted them to sound. Master photographer Tony Spina made me look better than I ever thought I could.

Production editor: Alice George
Content editor: Marty Hair
Copy editor: Kelly Feusse
Cover photograph: Tony Spina
Designer: Michele Vernon-Chesley

To my family, what else is there? My husband, my son, my parents and my sister — to those who came before me, those who are with me now, and those who are yet to be born.

1

CITY LIFE, CITY PEOPLE

Departing soul takes hearts along

FOR SOME REASON, THE TITLE OF WINNIE MANDELA'S AUTOBIO-graphy kept popping into my head.

A few years back, the wife of imprisoned South African freedom fighter Nelson Mandela wrote a stirring book: "Part of My Soul Went With Him."

There I was, sitting in a west side funeral home to pay my respects to lawyer Ken Cockrel, and the title of a book I never finished reading kept tugging at my heart.

Hmmm.

Ken Cockrel and I had known one another for years but we weren't best buddies, by anyone's stretch of the imagination.

I don't think we even had lunch together, but that didn't matter. Over the years, I watched him fight to make fairness and decency a part of the life of ordinary folks.

He always did it with flair. He was always pushing the system to its limits, trying, I reckon, to expand it so that it would include those it had shortchanged.

When he was fresh out of law school, he and other activist lawyers forced reform onto the Recorder's Court jury system by exposing the fact that the Wayne County Jury Commission excluded blacks, young people and women.

And it was also at that time that Cockrel called a judge a "racist, rogue, bandit, thief, pirate . . . honkie dog fool," and got away with it. I'll never forget how he defended his statement by saying that, in the vernacular of the streets, that's just what the judge was.

A few years later, he not only helped lead the battle to dismantle the controversial STRESS (Stop the Robberies-Enjoy Safe Streets) police decoy unit, he successfully defended a man charged with murder and assault in two shoot-outs in which one STRESS officer was killed and others were wounded.

Cockrel's defense was as bold as it was brilliant. He claimed self-defense for his client, arguing that STRESS officers were the guilty ones because they were all too eager to kill young black men.

Over the years, Cockrel fought with valor and brilliance for the causes I held dear. Because of that, I trusted him and I respected him. I valued his judgment and I was always tickled by the way he carried himself.

There he was, a brilliant lawyer, a charismatic community activist and

3

a former City Council member. He also was a fast-talking, easy-laughing, jive-strutting man who could hold his own with the best from Harvard Law School or the Brewster-Douglass housing projects.

He was a high school dropout who earned advanced degrees but never became uncomfortable on the streets.

You know, every now and then I'd see him jogging down West 7 Mile near his home. He always reminded me of a long-legged grasshopper, the way he bounded along, skinny as a rail and nothing but legs. Yet, he ran with ease, as if he had learned by hard experience where the broken pavement was and knew how to navigate his way around it.

U.S. Rep. John Conyers noticed the same thing. "He had this loping gait that was sort of like a street walk that was different from most of the people he associated with downtown," Conyers told a reporter. "He walked like a street guy. ... It was a definite style."

And it was. It was a reflection of his youth, an affirmation of his roots, and an undeniable testament to the fact that he still heard and understood the rhythms of his past.

If you look, you can see those rhythms in the exaggerated, rolling strides — or the jutted hips — of thousands of street-weary and street-wise black men and women everywhere, trying the best they can to survive.

It's a rhythm that says, "Pay attention to me. I am somebody special." And it's a movement that gives form to the unspoken vow of a people to be recognized, no matter what.

And I guess that's why that book title kept forcing its way into my mind in the funeral home.

In death, Kenny Cockrel took part of my history, part of myself, with him.

Ken Cockrel died April 25, 1989.

March 2, 1984

■

Crimes against city; where are the stats?

I HEARD SOME NUMBERS MENTIONED THAT SHOULD COME AS NO shock to any of us; still, they surprised me. The value of Detroit property — its property tax base — hasn't exactly been skyrocketing.

According to state figures, Oakland County's tax base went from $4.7 billion in 1970 to $14 billion in 1983; Macomb went from $2.7 billion to $7.7 billion; Wayne County, excluding Detroit, went from $6.2 billion to

4

$12.8 billion. Property in the City of Detroit went from $5.3 billion to $5.2 billon. (Some property on special tax rolls is excluded.)

A city tax official said it would be incorrect to say Detroit's property tax base is declining. Well, whatever the figures, Detroit wasn't exactly cruising in the fast lane during many of those years.

The discussion about taxes grew out of an exchange over crime in Detroit, particularly how crime is described and identified. Murder, rape, robbery, purse snatching — those are the crimes we are familiar with.

Other categories of crime may not hit you with the same physical force, but they'll get you just the same. How about a crime index that includes crimes against the City of Detroit, crimes by its residents and non-residents?

I'd start with a crime category that includes all the businesses that have left the city and moved to the suburbs. It would be unfair to single out any particular business; there have been so many, large and small. It would be unfair to single out three major department stores — one high-fashion, the other two full-service — that left Detroit practically high and dry for shopping. One of those stores had police troops stationed around its perimeter during the 1967 riot. I always thought that told you a lot about what really was important in Detroit.

Then let's have a crime category for those companies that not only left the city, but also had the gall to keep the city's name as part of theirs. Hair grooming schools, car parts shops, popcorn factories. Heck, if Detroit is good enough to share your name. . . .

Next, how about a category for those franchise restaurants that surround the city, draw customers from the city, but don't wander across 8 Mile or Telegraph or Alter with their cutesy cuisine?

Then add a crime category based on the fact that about two-thirds of black youths in Detroit are looking for work but unable to find any.

Let's lump "social" crimes in one category to include Detroit's black infant mortality rate, which is more than double the city's white infant mortality rate.

To this social crimes package add the 400,000 plus Detroiters — one-third of the city's population — who are getting some form of public assistance and the thousands of youngsters who drop out of school before graduation.

Oh, one of my favorites: How about a category for every Detroit student pushed through school from grade to grade without ever learning how to read or do simple math? Factor in some figure so this category will show if the kid's teacher sends his or her kids to a private school.

Let's make it a crime to have once-beautiful streets like Grand Boulevard lined from end to end with nursing homes and boarding homes where lost or aged souls are left for care. Maybe the crime rate here could increase every time a neighboring suburban or Detroit community

5

protests the construction of a foster care home in its midst.

Finally, let's make it a crime for former Detroiters — black and white — now living in the suburbs to tell people they live in Detroit. Add another notch in this category every time one of them starts talking about the good old days when Detroit was really Detroit.

I'll just bet you've got a few things you'd like to add.

March 5, 1984

■

Our miracle child gets little support

DUANE BRADLEY IS FOUR YEARS OLD AND HE HASN'T LEARNED TO read yet, so it really doesn't matter that he hasn't received any cards or get-well messages.

It really doesn't matter that his family hasn't received any messages from unknown friends, offering a prayer or a word of hope.

None of it matters, not a bit.

Duane's family is too busy wondering if he'll fully recover from the damage he suffered Feb. 23 when he fell into a swimming pool outside the west side Detroit apartment building where he lived.

The family also has been busy making funeral arrangements for Duane's mother, Mary Ann, who drowned when she jumped into the pool to try to save him.

Then there's the matter of Duane's older sister, Tamika, 7, who is staying with her aunt and uncle.

Tamika is doing just fine, her aunt said. The only problem is that she started crying when she saw Duane on television, lying in a hospital bed.

Duane's family didn't ask that this be written; they don't even know exactly why I've been bothering them. They've got more important things to think about, namely a four-year-old boy who is trying to regain his laughter, energy, spirit and mischief.

When I called Henry Ford Hospital, I wanted to find out how many letters and cards Duane had received. I thought there would be dozens, maybe hundreds.

After all, Duane is our very own miracle child who was pulled from that pool, more dead than alive. He had been under water for more than 20 minutes and he had no heartbeat when he got to Henry Ford Hospital.

The hospital hasn't exactly been overwhelmed with cards and calls for Duane. In fact, the nurses think he hasn't received any cards or letters from outsiders. But that's so difficult to accept and to believe that folks at

6

the hospital say there may have been a few cards.

Some parents who had children in the intensive-care ward with Duane have given him some stuffed animals, but they're just about the only ones who have taken time to show they care.

When another miracle child, four-year-old Jimmy Tonlewicz of Chicago, was pulled from Lake Michigan after being underwater for 20 minutes, the staff at Children's Memorial Hospital was hard pressed to handle the hundreds of cards he received. People who had never heard of Jimmy called just to say they were praying for him.

Jimmy's rescue was captured by a television crew and millions saw him pulled limp from the icy water; they saw a rescue team intent on trying to save that child's life.

The same kinds of people did the same things for Duane — surely their unspoken prayers were the same. The same intensity was there, the same hope.

Jimmy is out of the hospital and undergoing therapy at a center. He can walk and talk now. In fact, one of his doctors had to make Jimmy slow down because the boy got too tired roaming through the hospital ward.

Doctors here are waiting to see if Duane will regain all of his faculties. He's already regained his smile.

The two situations — Jimmy's and Duane's — are so similar. Both little boys survived. Though questions remain about how well they will be able to function, the mere fact that they are here is cause for rejoicing.

The similarity ends in our response to the boys. The frightening thought is that Jimmy's experience is more real to us because we saw it on television. And if it is more real, is it also more meaningful?

I hope not. But, as I said earlier, it really doesn't matter, one way or the other.

Duane couldn't read a card if he got one — he's only four.

March 7, 1984

■

Detroit area shows
Duane it has heart

YOU'RE A A TOUGH TOWN, DETROIT — A HARD-HEARTED, MIND-your-own business kind of place.

You've been battered by double-digit unemployment and assaulted by crimes against your inhabitants and your spirit. You've grown calluses as thick as a buffalo's hide after all the buffeting you've taken.

7

And yet, you — and people from Imlay City to Trenton — joined together this week in your concern for a four-year-old boy lying in a hospital bed, slowly recovering from the trauma he suffered last month when he fell into a swimming pool outside the apartment building where he lived.

The little boy is Duane Bradley. He was hospitalized after being underwater for more than 20 minutes. His mother, Mary Ann, drowned trying to save him.

As of Saturday, he hadn't received any cards from people outside the hospital — although a couple of community groups did call to ask what they could do.

On Monday, people learned that Duane and his family had not been inundated with cards and messages for him.

By Tuesday afternoon, the hospital received dozens of cards and letters for Duane. A huge Snoopy dog sat in a chair, near a tan bear that was nestled at the feet of a stuffed giraffe.

Some patients at Children's Hospital in Detroit made two colorful mobiles out of cardboard, pasted on pictures of animals and wrote get-well messages on them.

Youngsters from Brady Elementary School in Detroit stuffed a two-by-three foot paper heart with handmade get-well cards and trimmed the whole thing in bright red.

One little charmer added at the end of her message: "I think you're cute, too."

And then there were the letters and calls to the Free Press, as dozens of people offered help and prayers.

"When I heard about his mother jumping in to save him and she didn't survive, I choked up, because as a mother of two beautiful children . . . I have always been afraid when they were around water," wrote a Troy woman. "This could be me and mine — and I assure you I said a prayer, but also in our daily news, death is constant, especially in Detroit urban areas — everyone takes life so casually and it is a sin — it is also a sin to forget a small child."

A spokesman for a group of inmates at the State Prison of Southern Michigan at Jackson asked if they could help Duane in some fashion. It was the same question posed by people all around the Detroit area.

Some people who called or wrote said they hadn't forgotten about Duane. They had indeed said a prayer, but then, as one woman wrote, "I took for granted other people called and the hospital would say he's fine or just holding his own."

An earlier column about Duane mentioned a little boy from Chicago named Jimmy who was pulled from Lake Michigan after spending 20 minutes underwater. His rescue was captured by television cameras and he immediately began receiving cards and prayers from around the country.

I wrote then:

"The similarity ends in our response to the boys. The frightening thought is that Jimmy's experience is more real to us because we saw it on television. And if it is more real, is it also more meaningful?"

The answer to me is clear. You only have to listen to the calls coming in or read the letters or see the gifts and mail stacked on a table at Henry Ford Hospital to know that Duane is very real indeed to the residents of this tough old, mind-your-own business kind of town.

March 23, 1984

■

WCCC prexy lottery is a certain payoff

FORGET ABOUT TRYING TO HIT THE BIG TIME WITH THE MICHIGAN State Lottery. I've found a sure way to financial heaven.

I'm going to run for president of Wayne County Community College.

The way I figure it, once I convince the board of trustees to hire me, it'll be a piece of cake to get them to fire me.

Heck, they've had five different presidents in fewer than four years and they've fired three of them. So it shouldn't be too difficult for the trustees to find a way to oust me.

Then all I have to do is get a lawyer, go to court and sue 'em for every cent they're worth . . . uh, I mean sue them for every cent I can get. It's worked before, so why shouldn't I give it a fling?

After all, the board is looking for a new leader. Thomas Waters was named acting president in December 1983 after the board fired George Bell as president. But Waters was named to only a two-year term while a replacement is sought.

Just to be safe, I contacted two ex-presidents about my candidacy.

Reginald Wilson headed the college from 1971 until he was fired in 1980. He wound up with a $230,000 settlement, a plaque and a testimonial after he sued the board. Actually, a lot of people said Wilson was a pretty good administrator during most of his tenure. He was ousted after an audit revealed financial irregularities.

Wilson works in Washington, D.C., and seems happy.

His advice: "Don't spend a lot of money on your campaign."

The way he sees it, the board really doesn't care about qualifications or the lack of them in a president. They'll choose whomever they want and that's that.

9

Next I called Richard Simmons, president from January 1981 until his dismissal in June 1982. Simmons followed Wilson, although there was an interim president for a year.

Depending on whom you talk to, Simmons was fired for not solving problems fast enough or for being too independent. Simmons lost his $64,500-a-year job, but not his sense of humor.

When I asked if he'd serve on my campaign committee, all I heard was chuckling.

He didn't give me any advice about my candidacy. He couldn't stop laughing long enough to put two words together.

I tried to reach George Bell, who served from February 1983 to December 1983. I couldn't reach him at the college, where he was being paid his $74,000-a-year salary to work as an academic counselor.

I was going to ask Bell to be my campaign manager. After all, he was chairman of the board; he was president, and now he's fired. Who better to guide me?

I couldn't reach him, so I'll have to settle for my dad as campaign manager. He knows the workings of the downtown administrative office better than most people.

A retired plumber, he worked on the crew that built the downtown campus. He also attended classes there.

About five or six years after the school opened its doors as a truly bold and wonderful experiment in quality education for all people, my dad said he wanted to take some math classes but didn't know where to go.

I suggested WC3. He went there and took every math class he could find. I was so proud of him — and of that marvelous community college that allowed a man who hadn't finished high school to attend college with dignity.

He got all A's and now he can teach his grandson how to bait a fishhook, fix a leaky faucet and solve an algebraic equation.

The state is trying to set things right, and maybe they'll succeed.

But before they get it all fixed, I'm going to try to snare the presidency.

I'm so tired of ruining my nails scratching all those silly little lottery cards.

August 10, 1984

■

$9,000 question, and right answer

SOMETIMES GOOD GUYS FINISH FIRST.

10

Case in point: Dan Oden, 35, an unemployed East Detroit High School auto mechanics teacher who had been laid off nine months when he found $9,000 in old, unmarked bills lying in the parking lot of his Mt. Clemens apartment.

Oden scooped up some of the cash ("It took two seconds. I was real fast"), put it in the trunk of his car and spent the rest of the day trying to convince himself to keep the money and to accept the fact that he could never tell his son about it.

Oden weighed the pros and cons. He was going through a divorce, he had a son to support, he certainly could use the cash, and he was almost positive no one saw him pick up the money.

Finally, late in the day, Oden drove to his brother's home, plopped the money in the middle of the living room floor and told him what had happened. His brother, who had seen the evening news, told him the money must have come from the robbery of a bank next door to Oden's apartment complex. Some $140,000 had been taken.

Now mind you, after a full day of trying to act normal with $9,000 in his trunk and no job in sight, Oden found out the cash belonged to a bank.

It wasn't like finding a wallet or an envelope full of cash. In those cases, Oden said, he wouldn't have had a second thought. You give it back because it belongs to somebody, because you would want someone to do the same for you.

But a bank?

Oden's answer was, "Yes, a bank." He turned the money over to the state police (his brother-in-law is a state trooper). "Keeping it didn't feel right."

The next day, the FBI paid him a visit and asked permission to search his car and apartment. They had no suspects and, therefore, Dan Oden, good guy, was "suspect No. 1," or at least he thought he was.

"Every time I thought they weren't very thorough," he said, "they looked in exactly the spot I would have hidden the money if I had it.

"They'd do the nice-guy, bad-guy routine. Every so often they would say, 'What did you do with the rest of it?' "

Oden finally took a lie-detector test and passed. The feds continued searching for the robber, and the story was released to the media.

That was the beginning of Mr. Good Guy's introduction to public reaction. Some women wanted to know if he was interested in getting married again; lots of decent folks congratulated him on his honesty.

Then there were the other calls. Some people told him he was a fool or an idiot, and one person threatened his life. Oden considered changing his phone number.

By this time, he was sorry he ever had seen the money.

Then he got another phone call. This one came from a General Motors public relations staffer who told him to send in a resume. Maybe GM had

11

something for him.

Two months after finding the cash, Oden was in a training program for instructors at General Motors Institute. Eventually, he was teaching auto dealership mechanics how to repair transmissions.

The pay is better than the pay in his old teaching job; the benefits are better; classes are smaller, and the students want to be there.

"If I had known this would happen . . . that I'd get this job, I wouldn't have thought about keeping the money," he said after he finished one of his classes.

But he couldn't have known that back on the day he found the money. That's what makes Oden's story so special.

"I would like for people to know that if they do what is right, sometimes it turns out," he said.

That's something he can tell his kid.

July 1, 1985

■

Uncaring adults test
faith of brave youth

HURSHELL STROUD DIDN'T CALL ME. NEITHER DID HIS MOTHER, Mamie, nor his "lady friend," as he calls her.

The caller was a woman who knows the Stroud family and thought other folks should know them, too.

Hurshell Stroud, you see, is the previously unidentified passerby who leaped into a lagoon at Belle Isle to try to save a young boy from drowning.

The youngster, Kenneth Lamont Ray, and some of his pals had been offered $10 by a tall, skinny man to retrieve a model boat that stalled in the lagoon. Ray, 13, drowned after he stepped off a ledge into deep water and panicked.

The tall, skinny man got his boat from the other side of the lagoon, kept his $10 and left. He didn't try to help the struggling youngster; he didn't go for help; he said he couldn't swim and walked away.

Hurshell Stroud and his lady friend just happened to be at Belle Isle that evening. They were talking when he noticed something happening in the lagoon. Ray was bobbing up and down; another youngster, 15-year-old Terriance Davis, who also had gone after the boat, was trying to grab him.

Stroud ran into the water and headed for Ray. He told him to calm down, to tread water. When he tried to grab Ray, the panicky youngster pulled him under, the same way he had pulled Davis under. Stroud freed himself, came back to the surface and called for help to a tall, skinny man carrying a boat.

12

It was, he thinks, the same man who offered the kids 10 bucks. It was the same man who said he couldn't swim.

"He just looked down real hard at me," Stroud said. "I said, 'Go get some help.' " The man left.

Stroud pulled off his shirt and tried to use it as a lifeline, but that didn't work. He kept trying to reach Ray until it was too late. The boy slipped under the muddy water and didn't resurface.

Days later, Hurshell Stroud was reliving the incident.

"He didn't have any business drowning," he said as he sat at the dining room table in his Highland Park home. "I tried so hard. . . . He didn't have any business in the water. "

Stroud's mother was at Belle Isle that day. She was away from the lagoon area when the youngster drowned. When she returned, she learned what had happened.

Hurshell wanted to stay until divers found the body, but his mother insisted he go home. Before they left, she walked over to Terriance Davis and comforted him: "At least you tried. You extended yourself."

She has said the same thing, over and over again, to her son.

Still, he thinks that maybe, if he had pushed himself more, he could have saved the youngster. "But I tried as hard as I could," he said.

Hurshell Stroud is 15 years old.

He's a big kid, just over 6 feet tall. His parents are divorced and he lives with his mom, who manages an optical store. He's been on the honor roll since the ninth grade and wants to be a professional chef someday.

Before the incident, he thought that "adults were the ones who would help if something happened. . . . I thought they'd be the first ones to do something . . . not stand by and watch a child drown."

Now he's not so sure. His mother tells him there are a lot of good, caring people in the world; he just happened to run across the other kind.

Believe your mother, Hurshell Stroud. Believe the woman who comforted you, Terriance Davis.

She's right. She's got to be right.

August 23, 1985

■

Urban poem defuses
bus filled with rage

Blue is the violet,
Red is the rose.

I'm going to stick my fist
Up your nose.

Anyone who says Detroit isn't a city of poets has never ridden the DOT.

It was just after 4 p.m. and the bus was inching its way up Woodward. A disheveled young woman boarded the bus near Peterboro, I think.

I noticed her because she was carrying a large stick. Actually, it looked like a tree limb. It seemed rather an odd thing to bring on a bus, but those of us who ride the DOT have become accustomed to the unusual.

The woman had the tree limb in her left hand, bus fare in her right hand and a lighted cigarette in her mouth. When the bus driver told her to put out the cigarette, she ignored him and made her way to the middle of the bus.

He kept telling her to douse the cigarette and she continued to ignore him, all the while holding her tree limb. I was afraid that she would get so upset with the driver that she'd wallop the other passengers with that tree limb. A little smoke isn't that bad, I thought.

After repeated demands from the driver, the tree-limb lady doused the cigarette and kept the tree limb in an upright position. Then she did the most amazing thing: She stood in the middle of a crowded bus in the heart of Detroit and called the driver a nigger.

And, as if that six-letter noun weren't enough, she began embellishing it with a variety of colorful adjectives. I thought she was a little off center when she boarded the bus carrying a tree limb; I was convinced of it when she opened her mouth.

The driver shot her a look that can't be translated into words in a family newspaper; the passengers, the majority of whom were black, were momentarily stunned, and the tree-limb lady, who was white, silently made her way to a seat near the front of the bus.

"She's not a well person," I mumbled to my seatmate, a nice, older woman whose only earlier concern had been making her crosstown connection.

"She's sane enough to know that word," growled my seatmate. Then my seatmate reached into a bag, pulled out an umbrella and held it like an avenging sword. She let it be known that she was ready to give the tree-limb lady a swift and righteous taste of discipline. There was no excuse for using the "N-word."

I shut up.

The next thing I knew, someone yelled from the rear of the bus that Detroit is not South Africa. Another person offered the tree-limb lady a fairly innovative, though personal, suggestion on where she might put the branch. Insults came from all quarters.

It was quite a ride — nervous titters, lots of head-shaking and a searing rage that bounced off the passengers with each jolt of the bus. The tree-limb lady had enough sense to keep her mouth shut.

One male passenger kept repeating the "N-word," asking how the woman would dare say such a thing. His voice rose with his temper. He threatened her, yelled at her and, in the process, scared the living daylights out of a dear old white gentleman who had the misfortune of sitting beside the tree-limb lady.

Finally, the outraged male passenger coiled himself tight as a snake and stung the tree-limb lady with his verse. I confess I was too shocked at first to jot down the words; later I was laughing too hard to search for a pen. But rest assured, the spirit is here, if not the exact words.

Blue is the violet,
Red is the rose.
I'm going to stick my fist
Up your nose.

That four-line verse broke the tension, calmed the author and sent ripples of laughter through the bus. It imposed form on rage and gave a non-violent outlet to fury.

I left the bus fairly sure that the tree-limb lady wouldn't be harmed by anyone, other than herself.

Not bad for a little four-line verse recited by an urban poet in a moving theater.

March 5, 1986

■

She saw salvation in a city's rubbish

THE CIRCLE OF BLUE PAINT WAS MISSING FROM THE SIDEWALK — OR maybe it was just obscured by the mud and ice.

That circle had anchored an amazing collection of junk that once marched neatly down half a block of Beaubien near East Grand Boulevard, skipped across the street and paraded around a three-story house.

The collection included a wringer washer, a stove, a sweeper, building blocks, plastic bottles, fake flowers, raggedy dolls, tin cans, crates, boxes, jugs, jars, bricks and almost everything else that gets cycled out of our lives and onto the rubbish heap.

Neighbors called it an eyesore, but the soft-spoken slip of a woman who tended the collection once told me that she was God's messenger and was creating a shrine, built of trash. That shrine, she had said, would help save

15

all mankind from destruction.

The woman spent her days rearranging the elements in the shrine, painting various pieces, tidying up.

When her daily chores were completed, she ate dinner from trash cans — again, she said that was God's will — and then went to her unheated home, also filled and surrounded with the elements of man's salvation.

Neighbors said her strange behavior started at least 15 years ago. The woman told me that the idea for the shrine came to her in a divine revelation on Nov. 1, 1972. That also was the day when God and the Holy Ghost came down from heaven and presented a concert on the corner of Beaubien and Custer, she said.

It was, she told me, a lovely affair. Unfortunately, only she and a neighbor woman were allowed to witness it. But she sang a few bars from one of the songs for me and made it clear that tending to all that junk was hard work indeed.

Over the years, she had been ticketed repeatedly for littering, involuntarily hospitalized for psychiatric treatment and even jailed overnight. She gained notoriety outside of her immediate neighborhood when some artists — who did not have to live with the stench of the shrine nor the rats that scurried in and out of its mazes — decided that the little old woman's shrine was folk art and worthy of being preserved.

The old woman wasn't always God's personal messenger or a junk collector or a folk artist. Mizell Peeples, president of a local block club, said the woman was just like everyone else some 40 years ago when she and her husband and her son lived on Beaubien. She even belonged to the block club way back when.

Then, for some reason, she began collecting junk. There was no stopping her, Peeples said, adding that some folks feared she had supernatural powers she could use to punish those who opposed the shrine. Then the artists entered the picture and angered neighbors with their talk of folk art.

I never found out if the proponents of the folk art theory — including those who wanted to save the shrine from destruction — also wanted to provide the fragile woman with shelter and well-balanced meals served from a stove instead of a garbage can.

For the sake of harmony, I'll assume they did. But all of that is moot now. The old woman lives in a foster home, where it appears she is doing quite well, more interested in preaching God's word than in tending His shrine.

A judge who saw her last week said she willingly gave the city permission to clear away the debris. It marked, he said, the end of an era.

Neighbors who watched the huge trucks remove the junk also were happy to see the era come to an end.

As for me, I'm glad she's safe and that the eyesore is gone.

16

But I do miss the blue circle of paint.

You see, when I visited her last spring, she pointed to the circle and told me God had put it there. She said it wasn't a circle at all, but a tree into which the sky had poured its color.

June 16, 1986

■

People help people;
at least some did

SOMETIMES YOU GET LUCKY.

Karl Young thought someone should know what happened last Monday morning in downtown Detroit, and so the Detroit schoolteacher wrote me a letter.

Young was on his way to work at Tappan Middle School when he saw three young thugs knock down a young man and "laughingly" take all the money from his wallet. The thugs didn't try to run or hide, and no one tried to help the victim.

Young looked for a phone booth or a police car, but could find neither. He said the punks counted the money on the street, laughing all the while.

The thugs finally noticed Young and slowly began moving toward him. Just then Young's bus pulled up and he climbed aboard.

Young told the driver what had happened. The driver looked out of his rearview mirror and saw . . . well, let's let the driver, Lee Greenwood, pick up the story.

"I saw three men surrounding another young man. One took a swing at him, one held a knife on him and one snatched the jacket off and they ran toward Capitol Park.

"I put the coach in park and ran after them, down an alley and into the park. I caught up with them and said, 'What do you think you're doing? Gimme that jacket.' I was just so upset to watch them take advantage of that kid.

"I knew one of them had a knife but something inside of me clicked and I just went after them. I'm a big guy and I guess they looked at me and decided to give the jacket back. Then they ran off.

"I gave the jacket back to the young man, who was wandering around in a daze." Then Greenwood got back on the bus and completed his scheduled run.

Greenwood, 35, didn't tell anyone what had happened. He just put in the rest of his day and went home to his wife and four daughters.

If Karl Young hadn't taken time to write his letter, only a few people

17

would know about this regular guy, a hardworking father and husband who not only stood up to a bunch of thieves, but chased them down.

Even Greenwood's wife, Beverly, didn't know about the episode. "I didn't think I had done anything spectacular. I just felt it was something I should have done."

It wasn't the first time Greenwood went after a thief. Several years ago he saw a mugger snatch some keys from a woman waiting for his bus. Greenwood drove the bus down an alley, through a parking lot and across a major street in pursuit of the thief. He finally caught him and held him for police.

And it's not the first time he's helped others along his route. For instance, there was the time, back in 1981, when Greenwood was driving the Crosstown line around 5 a.m. and saw a woman trying to jump from an overpass. He stopped the bus and grabbed her as she started to leap onto the freeway. A few years before that, Greenwood saw a man having a heart attack on the street. Greenwood waited a little while for police and then put the man into the bus and drove him to the hospital. The man lived.

Greenwood, who was born in Detroit, can't stop getting involved in other people's problems.

"Something just clicks inside. . . . I think it's just natural for someone to help someone."

And that brings me back to the letter that prompted this column. While Karl Young was trying to get help that morning, a young woman who was deeply moved by his compassion and concern took time to give him the following advice:

" 'Why don't you get on your bus, go to your job and mind your own damned business?' "

Oh, well, no one ever said women can't be jerks, too.

July 7, 1986

■

Gas stations peddle
the seeds of death

REGULAR GASOLINE COSTS 77.9 CENTS A GALLON AT A SELF-SERVE gas station just north of downtown Detroit.

A water pipe costs $7. Baking soda sells for a buck, and the measuring spoons, gram scales and mannitol didn't have prices on them — or at least I couldn't see the prices through the thick glass window separating the buyers from the sellers.

18

Up the street and around the corner, the gas costs a few pennies more but the drug paraphernalia costs about the same. It's also displayed in the same open manner, near the chips and candy and milk.

Drive up to any number of gas stations in our fair city — or send your kid up there to get a loaf of bread or carton of milk. You can buy almost all the paraphernalia you need to get high — and maybe dead — on illegal drugs.

The cocaine accessory shop has arrived in Detroit. Head shops have been replaced by dozens of neighborhood gas stations that are raking in big bucks from the sale of drug paraphernalia.

These gas stations have it all — water pipes, chemicals that are used to cut or dilute cocaine, plastic wrappers to seal the dope, scales to weigh it and ingredients used to manufacture crack.

In case you've been on another planet lately, crack is a potent and deadly form of cocaine. It causes a quick, intense rush and is said to be almost immediately addictive. Heroin addicts say crack is dangerous stuff.

Well, the gas stations are peddling these accessories for addiction out in the open. And it's all perfectly legal, just as long as a seller gets a license from the City of Detroit.

The only thing they can't sell is cocaine itself, or heroin or hashish or opium or pot or hypodermic needles. To do that, my pet, would be illegal, and the merchants who are making a tidy profit from drug abuse and addiction certainly don't want to do anything that would cut (pardon the pun) into their lucrative business.

The Michigan Chronicle recently interviewed a gas station owner who said he would have to lay off employees were he to stop selling drug paraphernalia.

And Esther Shapiro, head of the city's Consumer Affairs Office, said the drug accessory business apparently is enormously profitable. "We've had hearings where licenses were revoked and (the operators) came in and fought like crazy. . . . They said they'd have to lay off people because of diminished revenue."

About 50 places in the city have licenses for "marketing items designed for use with illegally possessed controlled substances," Shapiro said. She said the number was higher until "someone" realized it is illegal to sell the stuff at places where alcoholic beverages are sold. When that happened, Shapiro said, the paraphernalia business moved out of the party store and into the gas station.

Talk about insanity.

There is no valid reason, none at all, for legalizing the sale of items used to facilitate drug abuse. So what if outlawing the sale of this junk would merely push the merchants underground? Some would say that's where they belong. Anyway, better underground than out in the open, where paraphernalia dealers send the clear and unmistakable message to our children that taking drugs is an acceptable practice.

City Council members are trying to come up with a way to get a handle on the problem. All I can say is that they had better do something quick, before we see gasoline price wars replaced by paraphernalia price wars.

The slogan will be: Buy the workings for one high and get a second set free.

September 26, 1986

■

Sidewalk sojourner guards her privacy

IT'S HARD TO DECIDE WHAT WAS MORE INTERESTING: WATCHING the woman and her four dogs share breakfast in front of the place where justice is dispensed or watching the people walk past the woman without seeming to notice her.

Even in Detroit, with its substantial tribe of urban nomads who live out of shopping bags or grocery carts, the woman warranted a second glance.

She had camped directly in front of the 36th District Court building on Madison. Her four dogs — three little brown mutts and a sleek black female with carmel-colored dots over her eyes — nestled at her feet. Each dog wore a leash of old rags.

The woman's belongings were crammed into an upright shopping cart. She had some empty pop cans in a plastic bag and what appeared to be old blankets and papers, and heaven only knows what else.

The five of them seemed perfectly content that morning. The woman wore slacks and sandals, a warm jacket and gaily colored head scarf. Her hair was gathered into a long wiry ponytail streaked with gray. Her face was peaceful, except for her almond-shaped eyes, which seemed to ask a question I couldn't understand.

The dogs were well-mannered. The big one slept curled up. A scrappy brown thing with a long nose and an even longer tail climbed over and through and around the other animals.

The woman drank coffee from a Styrofoam cup and ate a sweet roll she had pulled from a paper bag. Every now and then, she would break off a piece of the sweet roll and feed it to one of the dogs. Every now and then, she would dunk a piece of pastry into her coffee and share it with her pets.

She was a woman who kept her own counsel. She didn't preach her version of salvation to the passersby. She didn't rail at some unseen tormentor. She didn't sing or beg for money.

She just sat there, in front of the hall where justice is dispensed, eating

20

breakfast with the dogs. When she finished eating, she picked up the trash from the meal and stuffed it in her cart.

A lot of people looked right through her. They walked straight and fast into the building as if she didn't exist. A few people noticed her when they reached the corner of the building, but shifted their eyes into safe space before they had to acknowledge her.

Some folks did a double take. A few, including a young police officer, looked briefly with obvious concern.

After about 30 minutes, I lassoed a friend and we walked over to the woman with the question-mark eyes and the peaceful dogs.

"Hi there," I said. "I've been watching your dogs. They're real nice animals."

She smiled and said hello, and peered at me through those almond eyes. She used to have nine dogs, she said, but now she has only these four. Something bad happened to the others, but I couldn't make out what the nature of the calamity was.

She said she had some legal business to attend to and needed a lawyer. The courthouse seemed a logical place to find one.

"Where did you stay last night?" I asked.

"With my man," she said matter-of-factly. "Where did you stay?"

"With my man," I replied. She accepted that as a reasonable answer. I tried again: "Do you have anyplace to stay tonight?"

"What do you have in mind? Why do you ask? What can you do?"

"Not much," I said. "I was just wondering if you need some help."

Her eyes repeated the question: If I do, what can you do?

I left her sitting there. I could have called someone, but I didn't. It was warm. She was dressed. The dogs weren't bothering anyone and she was minding her own business, until I butted in.

I don't know if I did the right thing. Maybe someone else "got help" for her that day. Maybe not. When I checked back next morning, she was gone.

May 15, 1987

■

Visit to museum
good for the soul

IT IS SIMPLY SPECTACULAR.

A friend had warned me before my visit that I would be struck by the power and the beauty of the place. But she didn't tell me that visions and sounds from the museum would haunt me long after I left, that they would

21

brush against my cheek like gentle winds floating through time.

She didn't tell me that I would step jarringly into the past and catch my breath at the sight of a life-sized sculpture of a woman lying on her back in the hold of the slave ship.

She didn't tell me that I would lock eyes with the woman and be unable to move until she drew me closer.

She didn't tell me that the shadow of a chain would fall across the woman's naked breast.

She didn't tell me that the sounds of the ocean slapping against a wooden slave ship would blend with the moans of the human cargo, and that the noises would crash over me like waves.

She didn't tell me that my soul would cross the barriers of time and space and slip inside the shackled body, that tears would well up in my eyes.

All she told me was that the Museum of African American History would make me proud. Maybe that's all I should tell you about the museum at Frederick Douglass and Brush in the Cultural Center.

Maybe all I should say is: Visit the museum, take time to walk slowly through the exhibits, savor them, allow yourself to be captivated by them.

It is a rare experience.

Round a corner and stumble into the dark hold of a slave ship.

Stand in front of grainy pictures of slaves working on plantations and hear the sounds of the slave ship coming from behind you while the strains of Billie Holiday's "God Bless the Child" float from the next exhibit.

Read the Emancipation Proclamation. Read it carefully, word by word.

Return to the replica of the slave ship, look at a diagram that shows how hundreds of people were wedged, shoulder to shoulder, into that foul dark space.

My friend was right. You will be humbled by the courage of those who fought for freedom. You will be uplifted by the triumphant spirit that could not be shackled.

You will be proud.

You will also understand why Dr. Charles Wright, the person who gave birth to the idea of the museum, fought with such intransigence for his dream.

Wright had a vision of what the museum should be — and God help those who needed glasses to see it. Wright is an obstetrician and gynecologist, not an ophthalmologist. He grew impatient with those who did not share his vision, a stubborn, determined, unrelenting man, a man possessed by a dream.

But without that spirit, we would not have the museum today.

Wright and the museum backers spent 22 years gathering support and money. Donations trickled in at first. Then, slowly, the pace increased as more people realized the value of Wright's obsession.

The City of Detroit contributed $3.5 million in block grant funds for construction of the building.

It was money well spent.

■

Don't it make your brown eyes blue?

WHEN I WAS 13 YEARS OLD, I WANTED TO BE WHITE. TO BE PRECISE, I wanted to be able to step out of my black skin — whenever it suited me — and to greet the world as a blue-eyed blonde.

I never asked any of my little white friends if they wanted to be black. Heck, it was a dumb question. Black folks were rubbing bleaching cream into their skin at night. Black girls were making excuses to get out of swimming class so their freshly pressed hair wouldn't get nappy and "go back" — as in, back to Africa.

More than one black parent warned a child to "think about your children" when choosing a mate. Translated, that meant: Don't marry some dark-skinned person and have black children.

Black was a four-letter word.

But times have changed. Strong features, springy hair, earth-tone skin are valued these days, and that is good.

Recently, though, it seems that something odd is happening. Blue-eyed black folks — or green-eyed black folks — are popping up all over. That color combination used to be a rarity among blacks.

Today, entertainers, professionals and homemakers are shelling out some $250 to buy contact lenses that literally turn their brown eyes blue or green or aqua or hazel.

Wesley-Jessen of Chicago has come out with contacts that allow you to change eye color as easily as you can change your clothes. Called DuraSoft Colors, the contacts have been on the market in the United States since November. Already, about 300,000 pairs have been sold.

Nationwide, the most popular color is blue, with green running a close second, said a Wesley-Jessen employee. Hazel, the newest addition to the line, is selling faster than Wesley-Jessen ever dreamed.

The Wesley-Jessen people did some market surveys before they came out with the product. Of 400 women questioned, about 200 said they were interested in changing their eye color. Blue contacts got the most votes. Brown ones got few, if any, votes.

"In general," the Wesley-Jessen market expert said, "people born with blue or green eyes are satisfied." Apparently few blue-eyed darlings want to view the world through brown eyes.

How odd.

I wonder why so few people want to buy the kind of bewildered deep brown eyes that peered through the unholy darkness in the hold of a slave ship. Or the passionate deep brown eyes that stared down outward vestiges of racism in the South in the 1960s. Or even the terrified deep brown eyes that closed forever when the noose from a lynch mob turned black men into what songstress Billie Holiday called "bitter fruit" hanging from a tree.

But more than that, I wonder why so many black folks want blue or green eyes.

A psychiatrist friend (see, you knew all the time that I need help) offered two answers. She said blacks could be engaging in fantasy, trying to imitate American cultural values by becoming blue-eyed beauties.

On the other hand, my psychiatrist friend said, these green-eyed/blue-eyed brown folks may be fashion-conscious trend setters.

I have no idea what motive there is in each blue-eyed or green-eyed mahogany face I see.

All I know is those eyes remind me of a little girl who once wanted to step out of her skin.

July 8, 1987

■

Falcons should feel right at home here

WELCOME TO DETROIT, LITTLE BIRDIES.

Ralph would welcome you too, but he's probably hiding in a corner of some hospital nursery teaching the newborns how to cuss.

Ralph was a seasoned reporter when I joined the Free Press staff back in the 1960s. He didn't like women, politicians, blacks, Hispanics, whites, men, priests, rabbis, ministers, copy editors, new reporters, businessmen, saints or men who displayed any affection for or appreciation of any of the above.

But most of all, as I recall, Ralph disliked pigeons. He would kick at them every time he walked through downtown. I don't know if Ralph ever made contact with any of the little critters, but I rather fancy he did.

For that reason, Ralph surely is delighted over the newest feathered additions to downtown Detroit: five baby peregrine falcons placed atop

24

the Guardian Building on Monday.

Bird fanciers hope the little brown fluff balls will come to love Detroit so much that they will call Detroit home and raise their children here.

With a little luck and a touch of myopia, the birds will view the tall buildings around the city as surrogate cliffs from which they can swoop down at speeds up to 180 m.p.h. and grab a pigeon or a sparrow or even a sea gull for lunch.

For centuries, these owl-sized birds lived in the high cliffs around places like northern Lake Michigan. But DDT and other pesticides darn near did the critters in. They were almost a memory by the 1960s, which, coincidentally, was around the time Ralph was kicking at pigeons in the park.

Hmm. I never thought of old Ralph as an ecologist, but I guess he was, in his way.

Now, a movement called the Peregrine Return Project is giving the birds a chance at life in the city as well as in remote areas. Actually, experts think the peregrines will fare better in the big city than in the wilderness because they won't have to battle their natural enemy, the great horned owl.

So, little birdies, welcome to my city.

You are lucky indeed to have been brought here.

First, though, please watch out for those big mirrored skyscraper windows that have lured a few of your cousins to untimely deaths or injury. Once you learn to fly, dear birdies, you will get to meet some wonderful people you would not find in other places.

For starters, there's Christina Onassis, a man who stands about 6 feet 3 inches tall and wanders around downtown Detroit in shorts and big floppy shoes. Most folks don't talk to him because he is so imposing, but he's really quite nice, particularly if you ask him about the movies or the opera or Jackie O.

Then there's Stella, who roams the streets of Greektown in her white nurse's uniform. Stella scares away elephants with her shrieks. It works. You won't find any elephants downtown.

Most folks think you will fly south for the winter. But if you decide to stay, glide on over to Harmonie Park and look at the handmade Christmas ornaments in the Detroit Artists Market.

If you tire of eating birds, try the perch and fried potato balls at the Pontchartrain Wine Cellars on Larned or the greens with chicken wings and rice at Chic Afrique on Woodward.

One final word of caution. We Detroiters really do try to put our best foot forward for visitors. Tens of thousands of suburbanites fill Greektown and Hart Plaza and Bricktown and the Warehouse District every weekend. Please, use a little self-control when you're flying over those areas.

Only Ralph would have you do anything else.

Note: Ralph Nelson died two months after this column was written. He was 72.

July 29, 1987

■

Dreamers stay;
dream has moved

THE COST OF JUST ONE HOUSE IN THE UPSCALE SECTION OF THIS year's Homearama Show would pay for nearly half the houses on most city blocks in Detroit.

Heck, in some areas of Detroit, the cost of one model home in Homearama's Stony Point subdivision would pay for every house on the block, with change left over.

This year's Homearama has a "moderately" priced section in Macomb Township where houses cost about $120,000 to $200,000 and an upscale section in Rochester where houses cost from $240,000 to $500,000, with most on display falling in the $400,000 range.

Both sections are really quite nice — but they should be for that money. The yards are landscaped and manicured with plump beds of flowers and well-pruned shrubbery.

Inside, the houses boast such features as two-story living rooms, balconies, dressing rooms the size of most bedrooms and kitchens almost too pretty to cook in.

Visiting either one of the Homearama sites really is a treat. Admission is only $4, and it's an easy way to step into a dream, if only for a few hours.

The only bad thing about stepping into a dream is that you eventually have to step out of it.

And, if you live in a place like Detroit or Flint or Benton Harbor or Melvindale, you wind up stepping back into cities that have been bruised and sometimes battered by economic hard times.

In a matter of minutes by freeway, you can go from a lovely subdivision in the middle of a field in the far suburbs to a suspected crack house in the middle of a tired block on the lower east side.

In a matter of minutes by freeway, you see the extremes of the American dream as it explodes in richness or collapses inward from the weight of unrealized hopes.

To be sure, hard times and poverty are not limited to the inner cities. And beautiful homes and six-figure incomes are not limited to the areas around Homearama.

But sometimes the mere appearance of a place — the way a neighborhood looks — is so jolting that appearance transcends reality.

26

And a neighborhood no longer is measured by what it is, but rather by what it appears to be.

There's a block of old frame houses near West Grand Boulevard and Grand River where property values really would have to stretch to reach the city average for single family homes.

But on that block, most residents can name their neighbors, up and down both sides of the street. And inside most homes, it's a good bet that the fireplace mantle is adorned with graduation pictures, baby pictures and plaques honoring service on church committees.

Up and down that block, houses are fortified with bars and steel doors and dead-bolt locks to keep out burglars. And when grown children come to visit from city and suburban areas where most neighbors are friendly strangers, the children wait on the porch while the locks unclick and the barred doors swing open.

And then they step inside the place where the dream was born — and then abandoned by its inheritors.

The block I'm talking about is on the west side. There are others, all over the city.

But who wants to buy a house in an old neighborhood — or a not-so-old one for that matter — where crime is rampant and kids sell dope and people are packed so closely together that a cool breeze can't make its way from the front door to the back window?

So what if the block has an old man who tells Bible stories to kids and a young woman who teaches them how to play softball?

Who wants to pay $4 to tour a place where the dreamers are still hanging on, even though the dream seems to have died?

November 18, 1987

■

Shopping in city might help Detroit

EMILY POST WOULD BE APPALLED.

Twice in one weekend, I found myself lecturing Detroit-based service groups about the folly of holding their special events in suburban meeting halls.

I was the kind of guest who insults the cook and then asks for a doggie bag.

In each case, the host group met at a suburban location that was close to major freeways and provided free parking. Convenience was the operative word.

27

While the groups certainly could have found someplace in Detroit to accommodate them, it was just easier to find a place in the suburbs.

How ironic.

Hundreds of thousands of people have fled Detroit for the suburbs, taking their money and their tax dollars with them. Gradually and inevitably the Detroit-based hotels, theaters and businesses closed down because a significant portion of the population had moved away.

Some fled the city because of crime, others because of racism, still others because they sought opportunity and convenience. Whatever the reason, folks moved out and pretty soon new businesses sprang up around them.

For those people who stayed in Detroit, either through choice or necessity, life has become a challenge. My suburban friends yawn over the opening of a major supermarket in their neighborhoods; I do handstands when a new Farmer Jack supermarket opens down the street.

Some folks in the northern suburbs are complaining that there's too much commercial development in their area. My son had to stop me from taking freshly baked cookies to the people who opened a Target department store on East 8 Mile in the City of Detroit.

During the summer Homearama Show, my friends and I walked through more than a dozen gorgeous six-figure homes in a new subdivision miles outside Detroit.

When we drove back to the city, we took a swing past the building boom in my neighborhood: a new police station and a new house. That home, according to city records, was the only single-family home for which a building permit was issued in a year.

Jobs, recreational facilities, shopping centers — far too many of these convenient necessities have moved to the suburbs, following the people who decided to flee Detroit.

That's not strange. What is strange is the fact that those of us still here go out of our way to deliver our money to those same suburbs. We seem to be saying: You can escape my city, you can escape my neighborhood, but you can't escape my money.

If Detroit is going to prosper, I told my hosts, then Detroiters have to start supporting city businesses, even if that makes life a bit less convenient.

The money we spend at a local store helps that store owner hire a neighborhood kid and, with luck, keeps that kid out of the clutches of a drug dealer.

The money we spend with local businesses props up our tax base and helps to improve our schools so that our children can compete successfully with the children in those suburbs where we rush to spend our checks.

It's all a matter of simple economics.

Detroiters need not spend every penny in the city. That's silly. But

Detroiters must become more aware of where and how we spend our money. We need to understand who really profits from that spending.

The benefits of a good education, made possible through a healthy tax base, will last a lot longer than the designer clothes we buy our kids at some upscale mall.

And that's what I told my hosts, after putting my feet under their table and stuffing my face with their food.

At least I didn't ask for a doggie bag.

May 16, 1988

■

Board member is
asleep at the wheel

I'VE ALWAYS HAD A SOFT SPOT IN MY HEART FOR DETROIT SCHOOL Board member Rose Mary Osborne because she is the only member willing to do the board's most emotionally draining work — lead expulsion hearings for kids who get in trouble.

Now, after talking with Osborne about the furor over her continued use of a board-paid driver to get to school meetings, I think the soft spot was in my head.

In a rambling conversation, Osborne:

■ Vowed that, if she cannot have her driver, she would stay away from all nighttime school functions, including board meetings, for the 2½ years remaining in her term.

■ Said the other female board members risk their lives by driving themselves at night in board-owned cars that frequently break down.

■ Threatened to move out to the suburbs and run against state Sen. Gil DiNello, D-East Detroit, who is pushing a bill to ban all school districts from providing cars and chauffeurs to board members.

■ Said she is not afraid of crime in Detroit or anyplace because she has a .38-caliber gun at home.

Osborne, along with board member Clara Rutherford, came under increasing criticism last week when state Treasurer Robert Bowman postponed the sale of $30 million in short-term notes to the school system because of continued use of drivers. The delay could force the financially strapped system into a payless payday on May 31.

Osborne has refused to compromise on the issue, even though others on the nine-member board have begun driving themselves to school functions in board cars.

29

Furthermore, she said she has had enough, both of Detroit and the school system.

"I'm not running for the board anymore, and we're getting out of Detroit as a family and leaving," she said. "I'll leave the city and move to the suburbs and get in DiNello's thing," where, she said, she could run against him and get paid a senator's salary for her work.

Osborne defended her use of a driver, saying that female board members "Mary (Blackmon), Gloria (Cobbin) and Edna (Bell), who drive at night are taking their lives in their hands" because board-owned cars break down.

"If something happens to a female, it's not going to be me." It doesn't make sense to take such risks when it's not your job, when "you're serving the community," she continued.

Although Osborne mentioned crime several times, she insisted the fear of crime has nothing to do with her demand for a driver. She said she's not afraid because crime can occur anyplace and because "I've got my .38" at home.

Osborne, who said she is partially blind in one eye, nixed the idea of taking a cab or riding in a car pool. She said she has been honest with her constituents about her use of a driver. "I said, 'If you don't want me to keep my driver, then don't vote for me.' "

She accused Bowman of grandstanding about the sale of the notes. She also disputed his claim that the board had promised to give up its drivers when it asked for short-term financial help. "We did not promise to give up the drivers," she said.

Osborne's vow to stop attending all nighttime meetings would not affect her involvement in expulsion hearings, which occur during the day. At those sessions, she listens to testimony from parents, students and administrators, and then recommends disciplinary action to the full board.

For years, she has been the only board member willing to sit through the sessions. She never pulls any punches about her reluctance to expel students, even weapon-toting ones.

Despite her willingness to do the board's dirty work, it's obvious that Osborne is now sitting on her brains in her chauffeur-driven car. And that's a tragedy for everyone, including the veteran board member.

To alleviate the problem, I humbly suggest that Osborne follow a bit of time-tested advice: "Don't put off until tomorrow what you can do today."

In other words, resign, Mrs. Osborne. Resign right now. Don't wait for next week or next month or next year or, heaven forbid, for Dec. 31, 1990, when your term expires.

Leave today. We can live without you.

Osborne remains on the school board as of April 1990.

30

Get-rich plan
just takes you for ride

SOMETIMES, PEOPLE ARE JUST PLAIN DUMBER THAN DIRT.

Honest. I never cease to be amazed at the mind-numbing stupidity that manifests itself when normally reasonable folks try to turn a fast buck.

Over the last four days, I have received at least five calls from people who have been asked by friends or relatives to "invest" in a scheme that promises to turn a $1,500 investment into $12,000 without any work, special skill or risk.

There's nothing new about this scheme. It was around last year, luring the greedy and the gullible. Now it's come back for a second time.

Basically, here's how it works:

A potential investor is invited to a private party where he or she is given the opportunity to buy a seat on an imaginary airplane for a very real $1,500. Would-be investors are told they can get their money back, just for the asking. Someone in the scheme always knows of someone else who made a killing.

Each airplane in this elaborate scheme has a pilot, two co-pilots, four crew members and eight passengers.

Participants pay the pilot to buy a seat on his or her plane. When the plane is full — when all eight seats are sold — the pilot pockets the $12,000 and the plane splits into two new planes.

The old co-pilots are promoted to pilots, each with his own plane. The crew members move up to co-pilot status and the passengers get promoted to crew members.

Eventually, even the lowliest passenger will rise to pilot and pocket the loot.

Well, that's a lot of bunk.

The schemes are bound to collapse because they require an astronomical number of participants to stay afloat, more participants than even a fleet of imaginary airplanes could carry.

According to state Attorney General Frank Kelley, if the planes split every other week, "at the end of one year, the scheme would require 536,870,912 passengers to keep 67,108,864 planes operating."

The scam would require every man, woman and child in the United States, the Soviet Union, Canada and Chile to buy a ticket. The passengers would have to invest more than $800 billion.

Even if old P.T. was right and there's a sucker born every minute, it would be hard to come up with enough suckers to fill the planes and keep

31

the scheme in the air.

Not only is the scheme dumb, it's illegal. Last year Kelley's office prosecuted three Detroit area people on charges of luring others into an illegal pyramid scheme. One person pleaded guilty and two cases are pending. The scheme was grounded, if you will, for months.

Now, it has returned, with a new and perverse twist.

According to Detroit Consumer Affairs Director Esther Shapiro, would-be investors are told that seats are sold only to black folks. I think of it as equal opportunity fraud. All over the city, white-collar professionals, city employees, retirees, teachers, fire fighters — you name them — are being induced to shell out $1,500 for a seat on that imaginary plane.

Oh, if you don't have the $1,500 to buy a seat on the plane, you can shell out $200 to buy a seat on — get this — the Underground Railroad. It's the same scam, only with a different name and a smaller entry fee.

Aside from the sheer stupidity of getting involved in such a scheme, I truly wonder what kind of fool would participate in the obscenity of a something-for-nothing scheme that panders off the magnificent accomplishments of the Underground Railroad, that network of decent human beings who helped hundreds of thousands of black people escape slavery.

But that's another question. I guess respect for your heritage takes a backseat, if you will, to respect for the almighty dollar. Similarly, common sense flies out the window when it comes to get-rich-quick schemes.

This warning probably won't do any good, but let me say it anyway. You don't get something for nothing in this world.

If a money-making venture sounds too good to be true, then that's exactly what it is — too good to be true.

May 27, 1988

■

As dumb as dirt?
That slanders soil

EARLIER THIS WEEK, I WOUND UP IN TROUBLE WITH A LOT OF FOLKS for writing about a scam that is spreading through much of the black community in Detroit.

In my retiring fashion, I began:

"Sometimes, people are just plain dumber than dirt."

Well, I apologize. After receiving scores of calls — perhaps two-thirds of them angry — I realize that I committed a serious error.

I did a disservice to dirt. Dirt is real. Dirt is noble. Dirt, or soil or earth, provides food and nutrients that allow trees and grass and grain and flowers to grow strong and healthy.

Those who engage in and promote pyramid schemes — regardless of their race — are setting up other people for a fall. People educated in universities and people educated in the streets can and have been — bite my tongue — struck temporarily dumb by the promise of big profits.

The latest Airplane, Train, Bus, People Mover and Underground Railroad schemes are based on convincing people to turn over their money, then getting out of the scam before it collapses. I'd call it a hustle, but then I'd get even more nasty letters.

People are making money. That's to be expected. Those who get in a pyramid scheme in the early stages usually can expect to turn, say, a $1,500 investment into $12,000 just by recruiting new investors.

But those who join later — and no one knows when "later" becomes "too late" — will lose money. These schemes can prosper only as long as there is a steady supply of new recruits — fresh capital — to keep them growing. Even if some who have made a profit reinvest in the plan — and that happens — it still needs new money and new investors.

This scheme, like all other pyramids, will reach a saturation point where perhaps thousands of late arrivals will lose their money. That may not happen in the first weeks or months, but it will happen.

There's another risk, too. Airplane is illegal. Participants, could, like three suburban people last summer, wind up charged with a felony and face a $10,000 fine or seven years in the slammer. Those three were not Detroiters and, by the way, they are not black.

The latest scheme is in Detroit and it focuses on blacks. But it is not limited to Detroit or to blacks. I have heard about pyramids in the Grosse Pointes and Birmingham suburbs and in Miami. The investments in those scams range, I am told, from $5,000 to $75,000.

And, Airplane is not the only scam that has been splashed across the media. The Diamond Mortgage scam, where 1,600 investors lost $47 million, was run by two suburban businessmen. Both were sentenced to prison. In another scam, a white woman from Farmington Hills faces jail for fleecing investors, many of them Polish, out of millions.

A scam is a scam is a scam, and it doesn't matter if the perpetrators are black, white, yellow or green. Let me be blunt: Just because someone believes white folks made money through this scam, that does not make it right for blacks — or anyone else — to participate.

This nation is rooted in a tradition of profiting at the expense of black people and poor people. That tradition will not die in my lifetime.

But that obscene tradition does not justify black-on-black or red-on-red or poor-on-poor economic crime.

In selling the current scheme, promoters minimize risks and downplay the illegality. Few people are told, or accept, the harsh truth: that a slew of investors must lose money for others to profit.

Many people call this just another of life's risks, one taken willingly by many people. But even that shouldn't justify engaging in and leading others into a plan that is bound to have more victims than winners. If the planes split every other week, it would require more than 500 million investors in a year to keep the scheme going. Heck, even if all the winners recycled, it would still require millions upon millions of investors.

At some point, the plane has to come down. And when that happens, it won't be an easy landing.

February 6, 1989

■

Band rides work, manners to Europe

BEAR WITH ME. THERE'S A LESSON TO BE LEARNED FROM THIS story.

Last year, the members of Spain Middle School's concert band faced the seemingly impossible task of raising $22,000 in five days. The band members and their families had spent months selling candy and dinners, washing cars and holding dances to pay for a trip to London, England, to play in an international band competition. Still, with all that work, the group had raised only half of what was needed.

As a last-ditch effort, band director Victoria Miller contacted newspapers and television stations for help. Well, money started pouring into the Detroit school. Within five days, the band received enough to pay for the London trip for the concert band and a Toronto trip for the school's marching band.

You probably already know this. What you also know, if you were among the thousands of contributors, is that the kids from that east side school shadowed by poverty and public housing projects didn't forget their manners — even if they did become international celebrities by winning first place.

Shortly after the group returned home, the students helped Miller send thank-you notes to thousands of contributors. The notes were mimeographed and sometimes the students misspelled the donor's name, but the thought was there.

That's the way Victoria Miller operates. She makes her kids work hard; she makes them pull together for common goals, and she makes them mind their P's and Q's as well as their sharps and flats.

The way Miller sees it, sending those notes helped the students to realize that thousands of good people from all over the state were cheering them on.

Well, after the smashing success in London, the Spain musicians were invited to perform in the 1989 international competition in Bern, Switzerland. The fund-raising efforts cranked into gear again last summer.

But this time, there was something extra.

In mid-December, the people who contributed to the London trip received a letter from Miller about the trip to Switzerland.

"Funding, of course, is a problem, but not an insurmountable one," the letter said. "Families know they are responsible for $200 per student. Fund-raising has been an almost daily activity since July: car washes, barbecue dinner sales, raffles, candy and candle sales, band calendar sales. ... A tremendous spirit has been generated. However, we ultimately will depend on individual donations to help us meet our goal. Last year, your help was crucial to our success. This year we would like to avoid the tension of last-minute fund-raising. ... Your generosity now would help us devote more time to preparing for the competition."

Once again, the students filled in the names and helped with the mailing.

Miller wasn't sure what the response would be, but she took a deep breath and sent the letters off anyway.

By the third week in January, that letter had generated another $10,500 in donations. Thank-you notes already are in the mail.

The Switzerland trip will cost about $76,000 and the band is still some $35,000 short of its goal. The fund-raising deadline is March 1.

But Miller is confident the kids will go to Switzerland just as she was confident they would go to London. "I tell the students that whatever they believe in can come true," she said. "I've told them to start saying right now that we'll make it to Switzerland."

I'm willing to bet they'll make it, just as I'm willing to bet that the original thank-you notes convinced hundreds of people to invest in the kids again.

And the lesson to be learned from this story? Good manners and good teachers will never go out of style.

February 8, 1989

■

Teen facing death
gets to live a wish

THERE ARE, I GUESS, YOUNGSTERS WHO APPROACH DEATH ON

angel's wings.

Missy Porter isn't one of them.

Missy, who is suffering a form of cancer that attacks the muscles and spreads rapidly through the body, is approaching death as you would expect a typical 16-year-old: wearing designer jeans, maroon fingernails and emotions that change as quickly as the latest styles.

If Missy had the patience of a martyr and the compassion of a saint, perhaps her impending death would be easier, somehow, to take. If she always radiated selfless love and understanding, perhaps you could find some measure of comfort, even peace, by looking into her huge dark eyes.

But Missy — whose given name is Montoya — radiates energy and impatience. One minute, the tiny Detroiter is filled with love and compassion; the next she's sizzling with anger.

When she's happy, her smile cradles the sun; when she's cross, her eyes roll like thunder before a storm.

She is 16. No more, no less. Nothing, not even the incredibly cruel stroke of bad luck that singled her out for this awful disease, can ever change that.

"Sometimes I wonder why I had to be the one to get cancer and not somebody else," she said. "Then sometimes I'm glad when I have cancer because I get all this."

"This" was an all-day shopping spree at Dearborn's Fairlane Town Center, courtesy of Make-A-Wish, a non-profit foundation that grants the wishes of children suffering with terminal and life-threatening illnesses.

Doctors discovered the cancer back in March. First there was an operation, then months of chemotherapy to control the disease that spread through her chest, neck and spine. Now, there are pills and more pills to dull the pain.

Missy's mother, Bette, said the doctors have done all they can for this beautiful wisp of a child who writes poetry to God, storms out of the room when she doesn't get her way and wears seven gold rings on her fingers.

And why shouldn't she? She's 16.

She is a child, not a saint; an adolescent, not an adult. Some ailing children ask Make-A-Wish for a trip to Disneyland or a meeting with a sports star. Missy just wanted to shop until she dropped, and that's what she did — she shopped until the adults with her dropped from exhaustion.

Accompanied by Detroit fire fighter Donald Johnson, who is chairman of the newly formed Detroit Make-A-Wish council, Missy shopped from 10:01 a.m., when she headed into her first store, until 2:30 p.m, when she stepped out of the mall, trailing bags and weary adults behind her.

She had pranced, preened, pouted, sulked, giggled, wiggled and nagged her way through nine different stores, collecting treasures: A real Gucci bag and change purse, Guess? jean outfits, a designer full-length black leather coat, a pair of black leather boots, a thin gold ring with a delicate diamond in heart-shaped setting, lingerie, three silky dresses with ruffles, dress pants and a pair of black patent-leather pumps.

The shopping spree had cost more than $2,000. In addition, the management of the mall gave her $300 in gift certificates.

The day was about as perfect as it gets for a 16-year-old who has to take adults along on her dream shopping spree.

Missy loved her leather coat, she tolerated the black patent-leather pumps her mother wanted her to buy, she modeled the polka-dot blue-jean outfit in the store and refused to try on any more dresses, no matter what.

When she finally returned home, her friends crowded into her dining room to see what she had bought. Missy, who minutes earlier had refused to try on another thing, modeled her new clothes and waited for approval to register in their eyes.

And when it did, her 16-year-old smile cradled the sun.

Montoya Porter died May 10 at her home. She had been shopping the day before.

May 12, 1989

■

Angelou's poem inspires listeners

EVERY NOW AND THEN, WHEN I'M OUT TALKING TO SOME GROUP IN the community, I'll whip out a poem from my purse and start reading it aloud.

Sometimes the poetry startles folks out of their daydreams; sometimes it whizzes right by those pleasantly vacant stares you get when you've talked too long.

But once in a while, that poem finds a kindred spirit in that audience. And when that happens, the poem and the listener unite, sound to smile, rhythm to heartbeat, line to life.

Over the years, that poem and I have remained steadfast friends. As I have taken on new experiences, it has taken on new meanings.

Now, it reminds me of a young girl I met earlier this year. The poem and the girl are high-spirited and impatient, quick to rage and quick to laugh. Both are lean and sassy, self-centered and sulky. And in their intensity, they are beautiful and pure, true to themselves and to what they should be. The poem is Maya Angelou's "Still I Rise."

You may write me down in history
With your bitter, twisted lies,
You may trod me in the very dirt
But still, like dust, I'll rise.

Does my sassiness upset you?
Why are you beset with gloom?
'Cause I walk like I've got oil wells
Pumping in my living room.
Just like moons and like suns,
With the certainty of tides,
Just like hopes springing high,
Still I'll rise.
Did you want to see me broken?
Bowed head and lowered eyes?
Shoulders falling down like teardrops,
Weakened by my soulful cries.
Does my haughtiness offend you?
Don't you take it awful hard
'Cause I laugh like I've got gold mines
Diggin' in my own backyard.
You may shoot me with your words,
You may cut me with your eyes,
You may kill me with your hatefulness,
But still, like air, I'll rise. . . .
Out of the huts of history's shame I rise.
Up from a past that's rooted in pain I rise. . . .
Leaving behind night of terror and fear / I rise
Into a daybreak that's wondrously clear / I rise.
Bringing the gifts that my ancestors gave
I am the dream and the hope of the slave.
I rise. / I rise. / I rise.

Three months ago I wrote about Montoya Porter, 16, who had a cancer that attacks muscles and spreads rapidly. The east side Detroiter went on a shopping spree at Fairlane mall, courtesy of Make-A-Wish Foundation.

I tagged along. When the day ended, I wrote: "If Missie had the patience of a martyr and the compassion of a saint, perhaps her impending death would be easier, somehow, to take. If she always radiated selfless love and understanding, perhaps you could find some measure of comfort, even peace, by looking into her huge dark eyes."

But Missie, with seven rings on her fingers and nails painted maroon, wouldn't let you off that easily.

She was a typical teenager, full of love and innocence one second and seething with anger the next. She could be moody and demanding or generous and insightful. She wrote poems to God and she craved designer jeans.

"She is 16," I wrote. "No more, no less. Nothing, not even the incredibly cruel stroke of bad luck that singled her out for this awful

38

disease, can ever change that."

Montoya Porter died at home Wednesday morning, May 10. She was still 16. Nothing ever changed that.

April 14, 1989

■

School circus
could charge admission

MY FRIEND VI WENT TO HER FIRST DETROIT BOARD OF EDUCATION meeting recently. Within 20 minutes of her arrival, she was digging frantically through her purse.

"I don't have any money with me," Vi said to a kindly older gentleman seated next to her. "I must have left my wallet at home," she whispered. "Do you think they take VISA?"

"Speak up!" snapped the man, a veteran of many board meetings. "I can't hear you. This is no time to whisper."

The man shouted so Vi could hear him. At the same time, a board member who had the floor was trying to make himself heard over the noise coming from some quarters of the audience.

Vi spoke a little louder.

"I forgot my wallet. Do you think they take VISA? What about checks?" she said. "I forgot my money."

The gentleman nodded vigorously.

"Money? Yeah, that's what it's about," he said, slapping his knee.

Then he explained to her how some board members, in their clumsy search for an interim superintendent to replace Schools Superintendent Arthur Jefferson, had indicated that they could get veteran educator John Porter to do the job for $1. Porter's real paycheck would be picked up by some outside outfit.

Seemed like a good deal for the ailing district, the man said. After all, the board still had to pay Jefferson.

Vi tried to interrupt. "Checks," she said. "Will they take a check?"

"Yep, that, too," the gentleman said, cupping his hands around his mouth and yelling into Vi's ear.

The idea of Porter's check coming from some outside group didn't sit too well with some board members and community folks, the man told her. Folks figured that the person who writes your check also gets first dibs on your loyalty. So the $1 idea was scrapped, and a tentative contract was drawn up offering Porter $109,000 a year, a car, a driver and pretty much the same stuff that Jefferson has right now.

39

Before the man could finish his remarks, someone in the audience shouted, "Shut up!" The gentleman snapped back from Vi like he'd touched a hot stove. "Don't have to be rude," he said.

"That wasn't me," Vi said. "I didn't say anything. That came from the woman down front. She was yelling at someone on the board."

Vi waited a few seconds. After the board members tabled the vote on Porter's proposed contract, Vi tried again to ask her question.

"I left my money at home," she said. "Can I give the guards something to hold until I return? What about my watch?"

The older gentleman shook his head. "This is nothing to watch. You should have been here a week ago."

Some people in the audience, he told her, had jumped up and down and shouted all over the place after the board voted to offer Porter the interim job. A minister had to remind folks that children were in the room.

"Now that was something to see," the gentleman said, shaking his head.

By this time, Vi was completely confused. The board members couldn't agree on the time of day, and some audience members were carrying on like they were at a ball game. She feared she would never get out of there.

"What about an IOU?" she screamed.

"IOU for what?" the gentleman asked.

"I don't have any money to pay the admission fee. The guards are going to arrest me any second. Will they take an IOU?"

The gentleman burst out laughing. "Admission?" he said. "Why, honey, why do you think I'm here? I'm a senior citizen, living on a fixed income. This is the best free show in town."

When Vi finally got back home, she told me she hit upon the way to wipe out the district's huge deficit.

"You can't sell tickets to the meetings," I said. "That's illegal."

"You don't need to sell tickets," she said. "You can get rich off a popcorn stand."

May 29, 1989

∎

Parents of many
have room for more

MARILYN SPENGLER HAS THE "EMPTY NEST" BLUES.

But what the Bay City homemaker calls "empty," others would call overflowing. Try packed. What about crawling with kids?

For the first time in 20 years, the Spengler household has fewer than

40

10 kids in it. Things just don't seem right.

Marilyn, 51, only has to do 10 to 12 loads of laundry twice a week. Come fall, the youngest of the seven still at home will be in school.

"There'll be nothing to do," she says. "After all, there's only so much house you can clean."

That's why she picked up the phone and called me. She had heard about infants exposed to AIDS who have to live in hospital wards because homes are hard to find for them.

She wanted to know how to get a child, maybe two. Honest.

Since 1967, Marilyn and her husband, Nelson, 56, have cared for about 260 foster children. Some stayed a few days, others stayed years. Six youngsters — two sisters, a sister and her two younger brothers and a 16-year-old girl who joined the family when she was seven weeks old — were adopted by the Spenglers.

Those six joined the couple's five biological children, only one of whom now lives at home.

The foster children have come to the Spengler house alone or in pairs, sometimes in threes and once, in sixes.

A few years back, they took in six brothers and sisters on an emergency basis. The number of children in the two-bathroom, six-bedroom house exploded to 15.

When Nelson got home that night from his job as a truck driver, he found a note on the kitchen counter warning him to step carefully. Youngsters were curled up in sleeping bags on the floor.

What did he do? He stepped carefully.

Right now, they don't have any foster children. The last three left about a month ago, and Marilyn says "the little kids" miss having a baby around the place.

Why do the Spenglers do it? They don't say; they don't need to.

For two-thirds of their married life, they have sheltered all kinds of kids — infants to teens, physically impaired children, white kids, black kids, abused, neglected and scared kids.

One of their adopted daughters is physically and mentally impaired. The couple's oldest adopted child, who is black, was greeted with hostility from a neighbor who later came to dote on her. An adopted son who had been abused as a baby refers to his surgical scars as "zippers."

Despite the fact that the couple have adopted some of their foster children, Marilyn says foster care is not meant for permanent placement: "Even if the children's home is not the greatest, if the parents have improved, if they have done what the court asked, it is unfair to keep their children from them."

She says this, knowing full well that not all foster children wind up living happily ever after. If you just want success stories, you wouldn't go into foster care, she says.

41

If you want to make big money, you shouldn't go into it, either.

Foster parents get about $12 per day per child with an annual clothing allowance of less than $250. The Spenglers get about the same daily stipend for the children they adopted under a government subsidy program.

But, believe me, no amount of money can make you put up with all the kids in that house.

On a recent Sunday, the place was a blur of moving bodies in all sizes, colors and ages. There were biological kids, adopted kids, kids by marriage, and grandkids.

Curiously, though, the house was peaceful. The dog slept easily in the middle of the floor, the kids asked permission to leave the dinner table.

"What's the hardest part about being a foster parent?" I asked, thinking Marilyn might mention something like getting things organized or sending the kids back to a bad home situation.

But Marilyn didn't mention any problems. In fact, in a way, she explained why she and Nelson have done this for so long.

"The hardest part," she said, "is waiting for the next child."

June 7, 1989

■

House cries out for r-e-p-a-i-r-s

THERE ARE NO TWO WAYS ABOUT IT.

Aretha Franklin ought to be ashamed of herself.

That's ashamed, as in A-S-H-A-M-E-D.

Motown's Ambassador of Soul is the absentee owner of a run-down, weather-beaten northwest Detroit house that neighbors say has been vacant for four or five years, maybe more.

She has allowed the two-story brick house to fester. The pride of the block before Franklin and her ex-husband, Ted White, bought it in 1967, it now sits empty on a lot overgrown with weeds and shrubbery.

The house is a mess. That's M-E-S-S. In the 19300 block of Sorrento near W. Outer Drive, it spoils an otherwise well-maintained block of houses — solid, middle-class homes that Detroiters point to with pride.

Neighbors say they have tried for years to get the Queen of Soul to clean up her act. But Franklin, who now lives in Bloomfield Hills, apparently has ignored them.

"I wish someone could force her to do something about it," said Herbert Bell, who lives down the street. "It makes our property look very bad. Those of us who are interested in the neighborhood have been trying everything we know to get something done.

"But I guess she thinks she's too good for us."

Last year, Bell offered to buy the house and fix it up. But according to him and real estate agent Gene Nero — the same agent who sold Franklin the house in 1967 — Franklin turned down the offer. The house is assessed at $21,300, which gives it market value of about $42,600.

"I offered $12,000 knowing that I would have to spend $30,000 to repair it," Bell said. "Her attorney said she wouldn't take a penny less than $50,000."

Nero said he has tried to convince Franklin to repair the place or let it go.

"It's just a shame," said Nero, a former Motown musician who has worked with Franklin. "I told her brother to, please, tell Aretha to dispose of the property.

"When I sold Aretha and Ted that house, it was gorgeous. Now it's destroyed. It's rained inside of it for years. It needs a new roof, the pipes are broken, the floor is buckled, the walls have holes in them and the lower basement is totally destroyed.

"I like Aretha, but this is terrible."

Nero said he has another buyer lined up but still hasn't heard from Franklin.

David Bennett, Franklin's attorney, wouldn't comment without Franklin's permission. He asked me to delay writing for a few days while he tried to reach her.

I guess he hadn't been listening to his radio. The story was all over the airwaves; it broke in the Detroit News. Now, I may do a lot of strange things, but I'm certainly not going to put off chasing a story that's already into its second wind.

Anyway, Franklin has had more than enough time to show a little R-E-S-P-E-C-T to her neighbors.

A little over a year ago, neighbors complained to city officials about the condition of the house. City inspectors found it to be open and dangerous. Condemnation proceedings were started, but they were stopped after the house was properly secured.

There's not a lot neighbors can do if the taxes are paid — they are — and the house is not open and dangerous, a city building official explained.

Neighbors said that, soon after a local television station ran a story on the house earlier this year, someone removed awnings that were hanging off the windows. But even with those improvements, the house is still an eyesore.

There's no excuse for this. Leaving the house in that sorry condition is an insult to a city that proudly calls Aretha Franklin its own.

In other words, Franklin's behavior is just plain tacky. And in this case, that's spelled A-R-E-T-H-A.

■

A house of charm
boxed in by dope

UNDER NORMAL CIRCUMSTANCES, I WOULDN'T DARE CALL THE TINY senior citizen by her first name.

But these aren't normal circumstances. At least, I'd like to believe they're not.

For more than 30 years, Gert has lived in the same small house on the narrow Detroit street. For more than 30 years, a tangle of flowers and ferns has spilled over Gert's front yard, marched whimsically through her home and then set up shop in the long narrow yard out back.

Gert — she asked me to call her by her first name — loves that house. It's cluttered, but clean and comfortable. The good china stays in a wooden chest in the dining room. Copper-colored wire baskets loaded with onions and potatoes vie with houseplants and spices for space in the kitchen. Oil paintings and charcoal sketches hang on the walls and peek out from stacks of papers.

One of the drawings shows a much younger Gert, a woman who was among the most sought-after artists models in town. For 20 or 30 years, serious students at some of the area's finest art schools sketched her face and arms and breasts, the curve of her stomach and lilt of her head.

If she wasn't posing, she was busy in her pottery studio.

At home, she and her husband, Jim, entertained their artist friends and stopped to chat on quiet evenings with their neighbors. Jim, a tall handsome man with a rakish smile, was a waiter at a downtown men's club. He encouraged her in her art and gently helped her to feel at ease among folks she considered society.

He brought his paycheck home every week and gave her a new car every other year. When she got paid, she bought him something nice to wear.

It was just the two of them, and that was enough.

Then Jim got sick and had to stay in the house for most of the last six years of his life. After his funeral, Gert returned alone to the little house.

She's been living there since. She's lonely, but she's not complaining. There's the mail carrier to talk to each morning. Every now and then, a woman from Gert's church stops by to take her shopping.

Then there's Jim, of course. Gert says he's still with her. Sometimes when she's watching TV, a wisp of Jim's cigar smoke floats though the room. Other odd things happen, too, but she's embarrassed to talk about them, lest someone think she's a dotty old woman.

44

I have no idea how old Gert really is. Age and specific dates are banned from her conversation. Ask her when such-and-such happened, and she just laughs at you. Then she chides you for trying to figure out how old she is.

In truth, her age doesn't matter. She's a lovely woman with a fine mind and lifetime of stories that tumble out seemingly unbidden when visitors come to call. Sometimes there are so many stories clamoring for attention that Gert apologizes, as if they were children showing off for company.

I guess it's obvious that I adore Gert. I've adored her since the day two or three years back when she dropped me a note, inviting me to an afternoon of lunch and poetry.

She's special. But, in truth, she's not that much different from most of Detroit's senior citizens who spent their lives playing by the rules and trying not to hurt anyone. Now they — and she — just want to live in peace.

Even though I'd like to believe the circumstances of Gert's present condition are abnormal, I know they're not.

You see, Gert's newest neighbor is a dope house. There's another one a few doors away from the new one. At night, kids brazenly hawk their drugs in the street. Customers knock on her door by mistake. That's why I'm not using her real name.

Gert doesn't know what to do or whom to trust. She's afraid of the dopers. She's afraid to call the police. She doesn't want to move from the house she loves.

And so she stays there, alone and often frightened, with only an occasional wisp of Jim's cigar smoke to comfort her.

September 4, 1989

■

Hasty judgments
from Downriver

MY FRIEND VI LEANED OVER THE KITCHEN TABLE, PEERED INTO MY eyes and asked me if I had the gift.

"What gift?" I asked. "Was I supposed to pick something up on the way over?"

"Stop teasing," she ordered. "You're from Downriver. I know you have the gift. Everyone down there does."

I had no idea what Vi was talking about.

"There's no point trying to keep it a secret," Vi hissed. "Those two

45

women from Wyandotte blew the lid off the tissue box last week when they said Suzanne DeLisle ought to be hanged."

I still didn't get it.

Vi tried to explain. "DeLisle's husband, Lawrence, is the man charged with murdering his four children by driving the family station wagon into the Detroit River in Wyandotte. He's also charged with trying to kill his wife, Suzanne, but she managed to escape from the submerged car.

"Police say the wife isn't a suspect. In fact, they have a taped confession where DeLisle supposedly admits he tried to murder the whole family."

"Strange case," I said. "But where's the gift come in?"

"Right here," Vi said. "Despite everything, Suzannne DeLisle is sticking by her husband. Just last week she went to court to back up his claim that a leg cramp made him accidentally accelerate the car. She still loves him.

"Anyway, the case is going to trial. It's going to be a while before the court decides on the truth of what happened.

"But you Downriver people already know the truth. You also know what should happen."

"And what's that?"

"Well, this crowd of gawkers outside the courthouse yelled out, 'Hang her!' as Suzanne DeLisle left after her husband's hearing," Vi said. "It seems to me that even you Downriver rats wouldn't be dumb enough to do that if you didn't have a special way of knowing something the rest of us don't."

"And that something is this mysterious gift, right?"

"Right," Vi said. "You have the gift of figuring out the truth by counting the number of tears a person sheds."

There was no stopping Vi.

"These two ladies from Wyandotte were in the crowd outside the courthouse that day," she said. "They spilled the beans. One said she knew the mother was guilty because she didn't see any tears coming from her. This other lady said practically the same thing and that she hoped both would hang.

"It's right there in black and white in your own paper," Vi said, shoving the Free Press under my nose.

Tears don't mean anything, I said. "Remember the woman who let her crack dealer rape her 13-year-old daughter to pay off a drug debt? She cried like a baby when she was sent to jail for life. Do her tears mean she was a good mother?"

Vi hesitated. "I guess not."

"What about Jim and Tammy Bakker?" I asked. "When the PTL collapsed from all that hanky-panky and wild spending, those two cried their makeup off. Is that supposed to mean they're honest and caring?"

Vi got the point. "But, tell me," she asked, "if those people who condemned Suzanne DeLisle don't have the gift, what do they have?"

"The technical name is carp syndrome," I said. "Downriver folks do a lot of fishing because they live near the water, and they believe fish is brain food. It makes you smart."

"What's that got to do with carp?" Vi asked.

"Well, carp is a weird fish that lives indirectly off of . . . well . . . human waste. No one's supposed to eat it, but some folks do anyway. I'll just bet that those yahoos outside the courthouse are a bunch of carp-eating fools. They eat those suckers, and then they get it."

"Get what?" Vi asked. "Carp syndrome?"

"Yeah, that's one name for it," I said. "Down home, we call it fish for brains."

September 13, 1989

■

Students suffer
in a textbook case

I WOULDN'T HAVE BELIEVED IT IF I HADN'T HEARD IT MYSELF. AND I wouldn't have heard it myself if I weren't a snoop.

So first, I want to apologize for my bad manners. Now, down to business.

The woman, the mother of a Mumford High School senior, can't understand what's going on at her son's school. She seems to be an intelligent enough person, surely as smart as a newspaper reporter or a high school administrator. But she's downright baffled by the way the school handles the distribution of textbooks.

Detroit Public Schools have been open for almost three weeks now. The students at Mumford have not received their books. Some students haven't received them because they haven't paid the $10 book rental fee. That I understand.

But the woman's son and other students who paid on time haven't received all of their books either. In the woman's case, her son is taking six classes. He has only one book.

Why?

Because the principal of Mumford High School is waiting for stability. That's right. Principal Robin Oden is waiting for classes to stabilize — until most scheduling changes have been made — before allowing students to get their books.

Oden explains his policy as if it were the most natural thing in the world. It's been in effect for at least three years, and he sees nothing wrong with it.

It avoids the hassle of exchanging books when a student's class has to be changed for whatever reason in the early weeks of school.

Under Oden's policy, you wait until everything is settled, and then you get your books. It's neat and efficient, and it's giving a gigantic headache to the mother who called me.

School board member Edna Bell didn't get a headache when asked about Oden's practice, but she sure did groan. She said she had never heard of a stabilization policy, and she's had two youngsters go through the public schools. Bell said that a check of most area superintendents — the administrators who oversee schools in the various regions of the school system — showed that they didn't support that practice either. Only one — Benjamin Bernoudy, who is Oden's superintendent — stood behind it.

According to the Mumford mom, it would make more sense to let the kids have the books when they pay for them. She acknowledges she's not an education expert, but she figures it's hard enough to keep kids interested in school without throwing unnecessary roadblocks in their path.

Oden defends his policy by saying textbooks are available in the classrooms. It's just that the kids can't take them home until things stabilize. That way, the books don't get lost.

But that's not what the mother was told when she spoke to an assistant principal about the problem. The assistant principal said books would not be distributed until around 60 percent of the students had paid the $10 book deposit fee.

When the mother asked about homework, the assistant principal said teachers are photocopying homework material for the youngsters.

I know this was said because — low-down scoundrel that I am — I was listening in on the phone. In fact, I asked her to call and speak to someone in authority because I could not believe that the books weren't being distributed.

When I fessed up and told Oden that I had eavesdropped on that conversation, he said the assistant principal was wrong. He said that students who had paid the book deposit fee should have their books by the end of the week. He said a memo to that effect went out just before he talked to me.

His plan makes so much sense to him that he cannot understand why I don't see the wisdom of his policy.

When I told him that I agree with the mom's position — and so apparently do most administrators — he sighed politely and then gave me up for a lost cause.

It is obvious, he said, that I am not a school principal.

■

Bullet resistant glass
doesn't wash

SOME THINGS IN LIFE ARE SO COMMONPLACE THAT WE DON'T EVEN notice how truly weird they are.

A few years back, I was riding in a cab someplace in the South. I think it was Atlanta. Anyway, when it came time to pay, I reached across the seat and handed the driver the money.

Then it hit me. There was no bullet-resistant glass separating us. No little window to slide the money through.

Just driver and me, and whatever mischief or goodwill we chose to engage in.

I was shocked, at first by the absence of the glass, and later by my reaction to its absence.

You know, we have made the most amazing accommodations to the eerie presence of bullet-resistant glass in our lives. It's almost as if we believe that it's the most natural thing in the world to have a 1¼-inch slab of glass or plastic standing between two people who are trying to communicate.

Sure, it's not every place. But it's in enough places to make a difference in our lives.

Go to the dry cleaners with a load of clothes. You don't just plop your things down on the counter and wait for the attendant to begin sorting them. You have to feed your clothes through an opening in the bullet-resistant glass that separates customer from employee. The opening is large enough for a pair of pants, but too small for a gun.

Your receipt is pushed at you through a smaller opening.

When it's time to pick up your clothes, the attendant doesn't hand them to you. He or she hangs them on a little rack in a little closet with one door on the customer side and a second door on the employee side.

The customer can't open the door on his side until the door on the employee side has been locked. It's almost as if the pressing of flesh would soil the freshly cleaned clothes.

Yet, during this bizarre transaction, the participants carry on the most normal of conversations. "How ya doing? How are the kids?"

And that's just at the dry cleaners.

The same thing happens at the gas station, the party store, the bank and the credit union. The last time I bought a pizza, I watched through bullet-resistant glass as it was pulled hot from the oven.

And I suddenly remembered another time, surely not that long ago, when the proprietor of my favorite pizza joint would give the little kids a pinch of mozzarella as they waited with their parents. Back then it seemed the freshly baked pizza smelled as good as it tasted.

But that was years ago. Today, those whiffs of bubbling cheese, tomato sauce and lightly browned crust have to come from my imagination because the aroma doesn't penetrate the glass.

The partitions allow for an exchange, but not contact. I give you money; you give me fast food, clean clothes, a money order, chewing gum, an appointment with the doctor or a hospital receipt.

I may commend you on your good work; you may tell me to "Have a nice day." But we don't shake hands at the conclusion of the transaction. At best, we smile through a clear bullet-resistant shield.

The owner of one of this area's larger bullet-resistant glass and plastic companies said the big push for the stuff started about 25 years ago. At first, business owners tried to make do with those little sliding pay windows that you could stick your whole hand through. But that wasn't safe enough, so the owners went to glass or plastic with a turntable in the middle.

"It's a sad thing to say," the glass company owner said, "but even hospitals have had to go for it." The man does business not just in the city, but all over the area. Macomb, Oakland, western Wayne counties.

Think about it. This has been going on for more than a generation.

And, while we have guarded our profits and our merchandise, we also have raised a generation of young people who do not think it's weird to do business through bullet-resistant glass.

October 6, 1989

■

Sensitive motels
let insomniacs rest

SOME BUSINESSPEOPLE ARE SO CONSIDERATE. IT MAKES MY LITTLE heart go pitty-pat when I think about all the little extras they provide in the name of good service.

Take, for example, those caring, sensitive entrepreneurs who cater to poor souls who suffer from sleep disorders.

Most folks wouldn't be compassionate enough to go out of their way to accommodate those among us who have trouble getting eight hours' shut-eye.

But some motel owners have been going the extra mile for a number of years. Their actions have not gone unnoticed by me. In fact, every time I

50

walk or drive by one of those establishments, I think I hear music.

Now, you may not have heard the singing, but surely you have seen the more obvious evidence of this concern for the sleepless. Just drive down any major artery and you can't miss it. Like scarlet badges of honor, these businesspeople display their compassion in bold letters:

"Rooms for rent, by day, week or hour."

Who but a saint would operate a hotel for insomniacs? Who but someone imbued with the milk of human kindness would refuse to charge the full rate to sleep-bereft souls?

Such magnanimity.

Now, some who are quick to jump to the wrong conclusion might think that those "rent by the hour" rooms have nothing to do with insomnia. Indeed, skeptics might even think the rooms are there to accommodate goldbrickers who slip away from work to take a nap in the afternoon.

Still others, heaven forbid, might assume that this rental property is sought out by prostitutes who conduct their business there.

Well, shame on those who would pollute the air with their evil notions.

Those motel rooms exist for the sole benefit of people who are trying to make up for a sleep deficit caused by insomnia.

And, if you don't believe me, why do you think that there are so many music therapists hanging around those places?

That's right. Music therapists. They are professionals, usually female, who have studied the art of singing soothing lullabies that send the most fidgety sleeper into the arms of Morpheus.

To be completely honest, I was not the first person to recognize the social significance of these music therapists. Their mission in life was brought to my attention in the mid-1970s by my son, the Seeker of Wisdom and Truth, who was about three or four then.

Such a wonderful, clear-eyed age.

Anyway, the kid and his dad were heading downtown when they passed through an area with quite a reputation for prostitution and drugs. It was late summer. Even though the sun was finally beginning to fade, its searing melody lingered on.

Something was happening downtown that evening. I don't remember what. But the streets and freeways were clogged with bumper-to-bumper traffic. My husband drove at a snail's pace, which gave my son a good view of the area.

Suddenly the Seeker started bouncing in his seat and pointing out the window. "Daddy, daddy, look!" he yelled, happy as a kid on Christmas morning. "The Pointer Sisters! The Pointer Sisters!" he shrieked, pointing a chubby little finger at a group of women standing on the street corner in neon clothes and platform heels.

Well, of course, they weren't the Pointer Sisters. But the dress was similar. And to a little boy who had no other frame of reference, the women could be only one thing: members of that wonderful singing group he had seen on TV.

When he happily shared his discovery with me, I had two choices: I could tell him that the women were independent or semi-independent salespeople, or I could smile and say: "Wow, those girls can really sing," while warning my husband in a grating whisper: "You better not have any autographs."

I decided to smile and whisper.

To this day, I cannot drive by a highly transient motel or look at neon-clad working woman without thinking: "Wow, those girls can really sing."

2
MY
WORLD

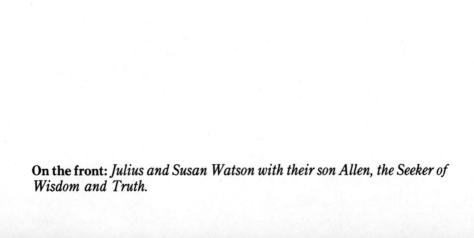

On the front: *Julius and Susan Watson with their son Allen, the Seeker of Wisdom and Truth.*

■

Piece of paper
transcends time

I HAD TO PICK UP A COPY OF MY BIRTH CERTIFICATE FROM THE Health Department Thursday. I thought I'd simply get a document proving I was born in this country and I don't lie about my age.

Boy, was I wrong.

What I got for my $10 was a trip back in time to a place I barely recall and a reminder of just how much that place and the people who lived there meant to me.

According to my birth certificate, I entered the world at 2 a.m. on a spring Wednesday in a little east side hospital that has long since closed its doors. Of course, I knew that.

What I didn't realize until I had the document in my hand was how very young my folks were when I was born. My mom was 24, and my dad was 25. My big sister, Jan, was all of 5½ years old, and she was hoping with all her heart for an elephant.

Back then, we lived in an upstairs flat in River Rouge, just down the street from the house where my mother was raised with her brother and sisters. Daddy was a laborer; Mom was a housewife.

The four of us lived in the shadow of World War II and in earshot of the trains rumbling along the tracks that divided our little town along racial lines.

The little house is still there, and I like to think that it holds memories of my parents when they were far younger than I am now.

How odd. At this moment I am 20 years older than my mother was when I was born. I'm 19 years older than my dad.

The birth certificate makes me feel as if I am living in two separate times — 1943 and now. Somehow I have become a generation older than my parents, who in their mid-20s seem much too young to carry the responsibility of raising two little girls.

I straddle two time periods and I see with time-warped clarity that my parents are only seven or eight years older than my teenage son, their grandson. They are peers, the three of them, and I have been left behind or ahead, both much older and much younger than all three.

I admit it. I have become obsessed by this $10 document. I ran my finger across the names of my young parents, and my eyes misted. I looked at their address and I suddenly saw myself as a little girl, climbing backward down a long flight of stairs.

I don't know why this piece of paper has affected me so.

Perhaps it is because I look at the birth certificate and I see two people whom I love, two people who have just taken one of the biggest challenges of their lives — me.

Perhaps it is because I have an unfair advantage on the young parents named on that piece of paper: I know what the future holds for them and I am buffeted by waves of joy and pain. I've skipped ahead thorough five decades of their lives while they are still trying to figure out a feeding schedule for a new baby girl who is allergic to cow's milk.

I know, for example, that my mom's life already is half over when I am born. She will live only 22 more years. I know that I am their last child. I know that my beautiful much older sister, described on the certificate as the first live born child, will become my beautiful much younger sister. She manages to slip into a corner and time zips by without touching her.

I also know that my folks finally will decide, after a bumpy marriage, that they are happier living apart than together. I know that I will bury my mother in one of her mother's favorite dresses. I know that my dad will stop smoking, remarry a wonderful woman and take up fishing and jogging in his retirement.

And I know I will give birth to a son that my mother will never live to see — a grandson who will make my father smile at the mention of his name.

But the two young people on this document know only that they are the parents of a second daughter, a cranky, red-faced ugly little thing that their 5½-year-old child gladly would trade for an elephant.

They have no way of knowing that someday that cranky red-faced, second-born child will herself become a parent and, at that moment, finally understand how very much her parents loved her — on that spring Wednesday morning and now.

October 4, 1985

∎

Is sexism turning into unsexism?

MY SON, THE SEEKER OF WISDOM AND TRUTH, NEVER FAILS TO remind me that I am older than dirt and incapable of understanding modern society.

It is to him a small miracle that I managed to survive before he entered my life. Without him to guide me, I would trip on my wrinkles and impale myself on my cane.

56

And so, this darling child of mine again saved me from myself. We were walking toward the television-stereo department at Hudson's Northland store when my tired old eyes focused on a pretty young woman standing near a radio display.

She wore a one-piece, full-length leotard, bikini exercise panties in a contrasting color, spike heels, dangly silver earrings and a shiny silver necklace.

She was demonstrating a high-tech disc player that costs about $225 and is supposed to produce a wonderfully clear sound. Several young men who requested demonstrations raved about the clarity and depth of the sound.

"Tell me," I asked, "why are you wearing that outfit to sell a fancy record player?" The model said all the demonstrators were given those outfits to wear.

I smiled sympathetically, sighed and dragged my son away from his continuing pursuit of Truth.

"Why did you have to ask her about her outfit?" the Seeker hissed. "No one else said anything."

I hung my head in shame. "I just wanted to know if it was her decision to dress like a cross between Wonder Woman and Jane Fonda," I said.

"It seems to me that, if women in bodysuits are going to sell trendy radios in a department frequented by young men, then men in shiny tights and plunging T-shirts soon will be handing out food samples at the supermarket," I told my son. The look in his eyes told me not to pursue the matter with Hudson's management.

Once again the Seeker of Wisdom and Truth saved me from making a fool of myself.

As the days passed, the episode slipped from my mind. I concentrated on learning to play polka music on the accordion pleats in my neck. I also tried to remember not to put the saltshaker in the refrigerator.

Then, I came across an item that brought back visions of bodysuits and bangles. The Playboy Club, long known for its fluffy-tailed bunnies, plans to add male bunnies, called rabbits, to its clubs. Playboy wants to attract women and couples, explained a company executive.

I was right, I thought; I wasn't seeing visions in my varicose veins. We soon will have men in shiny tights giving away Sizzlean snacks in front of the meat counter.

The story gave me the courage to call Hudson's about the bodysuit. So what if your son is appalled, croaked a voice inside my head, you'll never master the accordion, and refrigerated salt never hurt anybody.

I picked up the phone and got through to Hudson's public relations office. A pleasant woman explained that the model was wearing a unitard, the latest thing in unisex exercise and dance wear. The outfit is high tech to match the high-tech disc player; the silver bangles only heighten the overall effect.

Everyone knows that, she said.

I was so embarrassed that the gray strands in my hair began to blush. I should have listened to my son; he knew there was nothing sexist about bodysuits and bangles, bikini briefs and high heels.

If the truth be told, I could have figured that out, too — once I'd finished playing connect-the-dots with my liver spots.

April 13, 1984

■

No cookies baked, but no one starved

MY GRANDMOTHER IS 92 YEARS OLD AND SHE'S NEVER BAKED A cookie in her life.

Oh, she's made her share of hot gingerbread and fried peach pies, hand-cranked ice cream and homemade wine, but she has never baked cookies. Of that I am sure.

She, of course, denies it.

"You always say that," she told me last week. Gramma — her real name is Lora Jones Perry — had just come back after a long visit in Atlanta with her daughter Joyce.

We were sitting around the kitchen table at my Aunt Al's house. Gramma, Aunt Al, my Uncle Charles and me, snapping green beans for supper.

Charles was talking about his newest great-grandson, who is undoubtedly, according to him, the smartest and most handsome child in the world. That little boy is the fifth living generation for us — a fat-bottomed scamp who links the future and the past, even if it is on his knees.

Gramma looked up from her pile of beans and started talking about her children when they were babies. These were my aunts and my late uncle and my mother.

"I knew Bessie (that's Uncle Charles' wife) was ready to eat solid food when she snatched a piece of food off my plate when I was holding her. . . . Al used to go hide under the house. . . . They liked those cookies I made with sugar sprinkled on them. . . . "

Sugar-sprinkled cookies indeed. Those hands never pulled homemade cookies from any oven that I knew of. They did, however, raise seven children and sew and plant roses and string beans and tomatoes.

They stirred soup in cast-iron pots and were always ready to scoop up some vanilla ice cream for a grandchild. They gave nickels and pennies for

58

a bag of chips or some candy from the corner store.

They opened the front door and allowed a daughter or a son or a grandchild to come back home when life went sour on the outside.

They were gloved years ago when they attended the funerals of two of her children — her son, Bern, and my mother, Susie. They were gnarled last summer when they held her great-great-grandson for the first time.

Actually, when we drove out to see the baby, we didn't expect Gramma to come with us. It wasn't a particularly long drive but it involved getting up, getting out of the house, down the steps and into the car.

That's become something of an undertaking. But she came along and she sat in the car while we brought the child to her and carefully placed him in her arms.

She looked at him; he ignored her. Then she kissed him on the cheek, I think, maybe the forehead, and pronounced him a fine baby boy.

Don't get the idea that her welcome means she will ever bake a cookie for him. Far from it.

She undoubtedly did the same thing to all her grand- and great-grandbabies, and all that it meant was that you joined a long string of children who gave her enormous bear hugs while really trying to see if you could make your fingers touch behind her back.

It meant that you'd be able go to her house on Easter morning — the house her husband built — and find an Easter egg with your name on it in a fat straw basket on the dining room table.

It meant you could walk through the backyard with her and stop at the spot where Red, the family dog, was buried more than 30 years ago, and that you could stand in the kitchen and look up at the wooden star that Grandpa placed in the ceiling or go down in the basement where the memories of sawdust filtered over his carpentry tools.

It also meant that if you stayed at her house for a week, you'd have to eat Sunday's chicken — fried, then steamed, then smothered and finally hashed — every night until it was gone.

It meant, simply, that you were family.

Now, if our potbellied little cousin is very, very lucky, one day he'll hear my sweet-looking gramma with her curly gray hair and twinkling eyes tell him that she used to bake sugar-sprinkled cookies when his father's mother's mother was a baby.

Don't you believe it, kid.

■

Forever turned out to be 9 decades plus

I THOUGHT SHE WOULD LIVE FOREVER, BUT OF COURSE SHE DIDN'T.

She died on a Saturday afternoon, three days before Christmas, in a downriver hospital room overlooking a gray sky that eased into the river and settled there, silent and calm.

She died after suffering a stroke in the nursing home where she had lived for the last five months. She was rushed unconscious to the hospital, and she probably remained unconscious until her death, although she occasionally would open her eyes and let them wander around the room, trying to find something she understood, something she knew. She had lived too long to be a stranger in any land and yet there she was, trapped in a hospital room, unable to speak or to move.

She was 93 years old and she was my grandmother, my mother's mother, the freeborn child of a former slave. She was part of my life before I was born, and she anchored it every day of my existence. There was never a time before that Dec. 22 when I couldn't go to her and talk or hold her hand or just sit close, shoulder to shoulder, and understand that she was the source of my being.

I thought she would live forever, but of course she couldn't.

Lora Leona Jones was born in Alabama in 1891. She married my grandfather, Ransom Perry, who was a carpenter, and they, like untold numbers of other black people, moved north to start a new life, to plant their dream in new soil.

Her story really isn't that unusual, I guess. Marriage, seven children, their children, laughter, illness, perseverance, tragedy, a frame house my grandfather built on a small piece of land that turned into a gold and red and lavender canvas in the spring and summer . . . universal elements that may differ in texture but never in form.

Up until a few years ago, when she was well into her 80s, she kept house, tended her garden, cut her grass and scrubbed down the front porch, which stretched the width of the house she lived in for more than 50 years. But then, suddenly, the weight of her years settled upon her, slowing her step, dimming her vision, pulling down her body but never her will.

I thought she would live forever, but of course she couldn't.

Sometime during the last decade, my grandmother and I began this silly little ritual. Instead of saying "good-bye" to one another, I'd wish her a Merry Christmas and she'd wish me a Happy New Year. It started as a

60

joke and it continued for years. Merry Christmas in the middle of August, Happy New Year in April. Had we stopped to think about that peculiar farewell ceremony, we both would have known it was an attempt to ward off the inevitable, to push away time and force it to make room for another day.

But who stops to think about hidden meanings when you're saying Merry Christmas on the Fourth of July?

The last time I talked with my grandmother, I wished her Merry Christmas as I headed for the door. It was Thanksgiving Day. She had to be reminded to say Happy New Year but, once her memory was jogged, she laughed out loud about our silly ritual and wished me Happy New Year. Two weeks later she was in the hospital.

"You were lucky to have had her for so long," my friends have told me. And they're right, I know. But that doesn't fill the emptiness or erase the pain or explain how emptiness and pain can co-exist.

You see, the longer I had her, the more I loved her, and the more I loved her, the more I needed to believe that she would live forever . . . when, of course, she couldn't.

July 29, 1985

■

Grandkids can turn
tough dads to softies

MY FATHER USED TO BE A NORMAL PERSON. HE GOT UP, WENT TO work and scolded me and my sister when we needed it. He took us to the park as children and he sported a smile brighter than a rainbow when I got married in his living room.

All in all, daddy was a sane person, a solid citizen, a responsible human being who believed in hard work, discipline and fair play.

Then, his whole world turned upside down. I got pregnant with his first — and it turned out only — grandchild, and Mr. Responsible began the wondrous transformation into Mr. Silly Putty.

It started during the final months of my pregnancy. I left work about a month before the baby was due and stayed home reading and playing with the cat. Daddy, who was still working as a plumber back then, managed to get a job close to my home; every day he'd come over for 45 minutes of L&L; that's lunch and a lecture.

I'd sip tea while he delivered a lecture on parenting. Thou shalt not spoil this child. Thou shalt not pick up this child every time he cries. Thou shalt make this child work for a living.

When the Seeker of Wisdom and Truth finally arrived, my sober,

61

responsible, cautious, conservative daddy turned into a mushy six-letter word: Gramps.

He visited the hospital every day and never failed to comment on our good fortune in getting the best, the brightest, the cutest and the smartest baby in the nursery.

When we brought the baby home, he was there — marveling at every yawn, bragging about the size of the kid's fist and grinning from ear to ear over a smile induced by gastric distress.

Mr. Responsible stopped giving me lectures and instead spent his lunch hours discussing world affairs with a month-old baby. He also taught the kid how to eat a banana, how to stand up all by himself and finally, how to walk. Some might argue that the kid learned these things on his own; they'd be wrong.

Later he taught his grandchild how to bait a fishing hook and to fix a leaky faucet. Daddy went to all of his school programs, volunteered one year as a room helper and religiously attended every game when the Seeker played on the freshman football team. Listening to my dad, you would have thought his grandson was a cross between Mean Joe Greene and St. Francis of Assisi.

Suffice it to say, the relationship continues today.

I used to believe that my father was the only person afflicted with this strange malady that turns a normal human being into a quivering mass of silver dollars and giggles.

Not so. A coworker told me that her dad bought his just-turned-three-year-old grandson a sophisticated computer for Christmas. Not only could the child not type, he couldn't say his ABCs. My coworker's father got upset when the other family members teased him about his choice of Christmas gifts.

Another coworker has a beautiful blond grandchild named Emily who graces the office with her presence every now and then. You can always tell when Emily's visiting; her grandpa's eyes turn into thousand-watt light bulbs and the rest of the room becomes a backdrop for the two of them.

Poor grandfathers. They're such a silly lot. But they can't be blamed for their behavior. They suffer from a curious malady that affects only the male of the species; Grandpas get it; Grandmas don't.

And what a relief that is.

My godchild, Lacy, is expecting her first baby this fall. Lacy's mom has been so busy buying cute little outfits for the baby that she hasn't even begun thinking about the college my . . . uh . . . her grandchild will attend.

Oh, well. What are godmothers for? I'll just send off for a few college catalogs this evening, and maybe price some computers and put in a special order for a grandbaby's worth of bananas.

Daddy is better
than any celebrity

NO WAY COULD MY DADDY REALIZE HOW MUCH OUR LITTLE breakfast Sunday is going to cost me.

Even though it's daddy's turn to treat, I'm going to wind up in the red. Here's how it happened.

Alex Haley, the celebrity author who wrote "Autobiography of Malcolm X" and "Roots," is coming to town this weekend to speak at the Retirement Lifestyle Expo at Cobo Hall.

A friend, thinking I'd enjoy meeting Haley, wrangled me an invitation to have brunch with him and some local swells on Sunday.

For about half a second, I seriously considered taking her up on it. After all, with a little nerve, I could get Haley to autograph my copies of his books — maybe even dribble a little coffee on them to hint at the intimacy of the setting.

Then I'd steal a little bit of croissant off his plate and maybe a smidgeon of smoked salmon or ham or whatever you eat at a brunch. I'd take that stuff, seal it up tight in a plastic bag and sell the whole shebang at one of those fancy New York auctions.

Look, I read where someone paid for Michael Jackson's yellow rhinestone pants. Last year, another collector of things, not thoughts, paid $21,000 for two cookie jars and a set of salt and pepper shakers that belonged to Andy Warhol.

It was a sure bet that my Haley memorabilia — surely more intimate than a cookie jar and more relevant than yellow pants — would command enough money for me to spend a week in the Bahamas.

I could already feel sun toasting my shoulders when I remembered a previous engagement for Sunday: I have to refill my daddy's coffee cup.

You see, my daddy and I have this standing date for breakfast every Sunday morning at a little fast food restaurant just north of my house.

Daddy drives over in his van, picks me up, and off we go to join the other Sunday morning regulars — the retired factory worker/union activist/vegetarian/philosopher/social historian who recently moved from his home in Southfield to a smaller, more manageable place in a nearby suburb. The church ladies who come in all girdled and gussied up, trailing cologne and sharing bright red lipstick smiles. The little girl who has her daddy wrapped around one sweet baby finger and her mama wrapped around the other.

Our routine seldom varies. I place the order. Daddy and I take turns paying. We try not to forget the senior citizens discount. Daddy carries the tray. I refill the coffee cups.

We've been doing this for about a year now, maybe a little longer. We don't talk about anything special. Just stuff that comes to Daddy's mind.

Stuff like drawing water from a community well. Or using the dipper on a winter morning to break the crust of ice on the water bucket in the kitchen. Or working in the garden out back with his older brothers when he'd rather be listening to some mystery show on the radio in the parlor.

Stuff like seeing his dad, my grandpa, come home night after night in the winter, nearly frozen, from working outside at the factory without a chance to get warmed up.

Just stuff. Just a houseful of kids — my aunts and uncles — arguing over the corner piece from a pan of homemade biscuits, crunchy on top and soft as a warm buttered cloud in the middle.

Now, mind you, Daddy and I don't spend all our time talking about the past. There are politics and finances and anything from the papers that catches our fancy.

Then he drives me home and goes off to visit his brother, Kenny. I spend the rest of the day moving the dust from one spot to another and getting things ready for work the next day.

The way I figure it, breakfast costs about four bucks for the two of us. The Haley stuff could have netted me an easy $500.

And that means I'll owe my daddy exactly $496 Sunday morning — or maybe a little bit less if we forget the discount again.

April 21, 1989

■

And the truth will set you . . . on edge

EVERY ADULT WHO HAS EVER SPENT ANY TIME AROUND YOUNG children knows that the truth, when it comes from a toddler's mouth, doesn't set you free.

More often than not, it embarrasses you to tears.

And those who have fallen victim to the disarming candor of the very young know that it takes years before you fully recover from that burble of truth that demanded to be heard at the most inopportune time.

One of my dear friends still smarts whenever she thinks of the time her young son, no more than three, announced in a crowded supermarket that he just loved "big chestes." What he meant . . . well, you know what he meant.

A rather ample woman walking by had triggered his utterance, and nothing his mother could do would shut him up.

Now, some folks foolishly believe that these pint-sized peddlers of truth can't lie because they are too innocent or too pure to indulge in such duplicity.

But anyone who believes that obviously has never happened upon a baby with a smile straight from heaven and a diaper from hell.

No. Innocence and purity have nothing to do with it.

It's all about the inherent nature of lies and truth.

Lies are devious, ugly, slimy things that flourish in the dark corners of your mouth until they can slip out through the little spaces between your teeth. They crawl in their shadows across the floor.

The truth, on the other hand, thrives on light. It demands to be free. Place the truth in a dark hole and it will seek the sun the way a flower turns toward the light.

The simple truth of the matter is that little kids don't lie between their teeth because they can't. Period.

These snaggle-toothed, gap-toothed, tiny-toothed people don't have teeth to keep the truth from dashing into the light. That same dental affliction prevents the kids from providing a decent breeding ground for lies.

It's true. Let me give you an example.

Years ago, one of my little cousins, a lovely child who delighted in fairy tales, happened upon the most important find of her brief life.

My cousin was sitting on the front porch next to her grandmother when a neighbor lady stopped to say hello on her way to the store.

Well, the neighbor was kindly, with a good heart and a loving family.

But her laughter screeched like fingernails on a blackboard and her face was a study in odd angles and hairy protuberances. It didn't help much that she always wore dark shapeless dresses that just hung from her shoulders.

Well, my cousin took one look at the neighbor — I guess she had never noticed her before — and joyously announced in that tiny, piercing voice of hers: "Look, Grandma, she be the witch."

The little one was so happy to have found a real life witch that she couldn't stop staying, "She be the witch. She be the witch." When her poor grandmother tried to shush her, my cousin would have none of it. She stood directly in front of the kindly neighbor and, truth oozing through the space where teeth one day would be, sought affirmation from the source: "But you do be the witch, don't you, lady?"

Needless to say, the kindly neighbor headed off to the store, trailing dark oaths behind her about that ill-mannered child.

Now if the truth be told, that kindly neighbor did indeed look just like a witch. But no one would ever say that. We, with our teeth fully in place, talked about what a pleasant personality she had. We never failed to say that she looked mighty nice on Sunday mornings as she headed to church.

It was only in the safety of our home that we would toss back our heads, throw open our mouths and laugh ourselves silly about "you be the witch."

Still don't buy my theory of teeth and truth?

Well, just answer me this one question. Why do you think they call dentures false teeth?

September 25, 1985

■

Brilliant cover-up of a broken heart

I SAT UP THE NIGHT BEFORE, WONDERING WHAT I'D DO WHEN WE met again. It had been years since we last saw each other but I knew nothing had changed — at least on his part.

We were sweethearts, after a fashion — at least, as much sweethearts as you can be when your world is limited by the end of the block and all your explorations must end when the streetlights come on.

We had grown up together — kindergarten, junior high, high school. All during that time I was convinced he had a crush on me. I think it was because he gave me dime-store Valentine cards and flashed a snaggle-toothed grin on the playground.

We went our separate ways after high school. Occasionally, we bumped into each other but always in public places, always by accident. But this time, it would be different.

I decided that I would be kind at our meeting; I would be understanding and generous and gracious. I would do nothing to remind him of his unrequited love, nothing to cause him to curse the fate that had kept us apart.

After all, I'm a mature adult now, no longer a silly child.

Somehow, I knew I'd find a way to let him know that ours was a relationship that could never be. When I broke the news, and I would, I would be . . . gentle.

OK, I was weaned on schmaltzy movies. . . . Greer Garson oozing grace and determination, Deborah Kerr antiseptically encased in British-accented passion.

I arrived early; he arrived late. Poor baby, I thought. He probably sat in the car trying to summon the courage to enter. It must be difficult to be in the same room with a loved one and not be able to express emotion.

He walked down the stairs, flashed almost the same smile (he has all of his teeth now) and then did the most outrageous thing. He hugged and kissed almost every woman in the room.

He kissed Virginia and Brenda and Ronnie; he kissed Rosemary and Quintelle and heaven only knows whom else.

He laughed and joked, flashed that smile again and allowed as how he had loved us all. . . . Virginia in the second grade; me perhaps in the third.

"But I thought I was the only one," I said, suddenly finding myself in an echo chamber.

"Oh no," he laughed. "I loved you all."

Strange things happen when old friends from a small town get together again. About a dozen of my former classmates met that day to plan a reunion of our high school graduating class.

Huge chunks of our lives had been lopped off since we left River Rouge High School; yet, for me at least, we were instantly transformed into teenagers again — or maybe grade-schoolers, depending on whom you were talking to or expecting. We giggled, laughed about old flames and tried to conjure faces to fit names on a list of classmates.

We filled each other in on the intervening years and then swept those years outside where Rosemary's two kids were shooting hoops — where they both were told to stay until it was time for us to leave.

It was a magical afternoon. What made it even more special was the fact that after all those years the guy who adored me in grade school hadn't changed one bit. Even back then he would never have hurt anyone's feelings by singling out just one little girl for special attention. He had to say he loved us all; how could he do otherwise under the adoring eyes of a half-dozen females?

You know, I'll bet he, too, sat up the night before, wondering how to handle such a delicate situation.

February 13, 1985

■

Softly, poems sing
lessons of the past

I GREW UP LISTENING TO THE RHYTHMS OF PAUL LAURENCE Dunbar, the turn-of-the-century poet whose words carried me to places I had never seen but places I knew I belonged.

I grew up listening to my mother recite verse after verse of his warm sugar-cinnamon poems that bubbled and boiled and sizzled and then stuck

67

to my soul forever.

Dunbar, who lived from 1872 to 1906, was the son of former slaves and became one of the most popular poets of his time.

He wrote a few novels, some essays and lots of "standard" English poetry. But it was his special poems, his dialect works that I remember, his wonderful moving, jumping, thumping, sassy poems that captured the iron spirit and the humor of slaves and then preserved those images for us.

I wish you could have been introduced to Dunbar the way I was, in the kitchen near the stove while my mother cooked dinner and recited poetry all at the same time.

Chicken, spaghetti, Dunbar and greens; it wasn't a bad combination.

Sometimes there were other poems in the kitchen, long rambling pieces about heroic deeds or funny little ditties I think she embroidered as she went along. But it was Dunbar, the Dunbar of the slave cabin or the meeting hall or the secret gathering in the field, that my sister and I loved.

I started thinking about Dunbar after attending an exceptional conference at Detroit's Hartford Memorial Baptist Church. The theme was "Remnants of African Roots in American African Culture." During lunch, one of my tablemates creased her brow and fretted about the use of black English. She proudly allowed as how she learned to speak "proper" English and can't speak the other kind. People even mistake her for white — over the phone.

I said, "I been speaking it for years," and returned to my lunch. I wish I had thought then to tell her about Dunbar and the beautiful kitchen poems that helped introduce me to my heritage.

"Dey had a gread big pahty down to Tom's de othah night. . . . All de folks f'om fou' plantations was invited, an' dey come. . . . Gals all dressed in silks and satins, not a wrinkle ner a crease. . . . If you'd seen 'em wif deir mistus, couldn't swahed to which was which. . . ."

The poem is called "The Party," and it's one long feast of sound and smell and dance and laughter, a joyous song richer than silks and satins.

That's one side of Dunbar. There also is the Dunbar who used dialect to speak of justice in his classic "An Ante-Bellum Sermon."

"Now ole Pher'oh, down in Egypt,
Was the wuss man evah bo'n,
An' he had de Hebrew chillun
Down dah wukin in hi co'n . . .
'T well de Lawd got tiahed o' his foolin',
An' sez he: "I'll let him know
— Look hyeah, Moses, go tell Pher'oh
Fu' to let dem chillun go. . . .
Now de Lawd done dis fu Isrul,
An' his ways don't nevah change,

And the love he showed to Isrul
Wasn't all on Isrul spent . . .
Cose ole Pher'oh b'lieved in slav'ry
But de Lawd he let him see,
Dat de people he put bref in, —
Evah mothah's son was free. . . . "

And then's there's the Dunbar whose poetry provided the title for Maya Angelou's autobiography. Angelou called her brilliant creation: "I Know Why the Caged Bird Sings." Dunbar called his "Sympathy."

"I know what the caged bird feels, alas!
When the sun is bright on the upland slopes;
When the wind stirs soft through the springing grass,
And the river flows like a stream of glass. . . .
I know why the caged bird sings,
ah me,
When his wing is bruised and his bosom sore, —
When he beat his bars and he would be free;
It is not a carol of joy or glee,
But a plea, that upward to Heaven he flings —
I know why the caged bird sings!"

I hope my tablemate will learn some day both why — and how — the caged bird sang.

March 18, 1985

■

A breath of spring in legacy of a friend

THERE WILL COME A TIME, I SUPPOSE, WHEN THIS SEASON WHICH IS caught between winter and spring will pass without my thinking about her.

There will come a time, I know, when nature's tug-of-war won't remind me of her internal struggle. It's been seven years now since she died, but still I remember her on days like this, when the sky is clear and the sun is shining and a hint of spring softens the cold.

Last year around this time, the memories came after lunch with two college chums from the University of Michigan. The collective years we spent in school exceeded our individual ages — something we will not be able to say much longer — and we talked about old times and new concerns.

69

The lunch, I thought back then, would have been more fun had she been there. She had a way of catching the spin of the Earth on a lazy afternoon and taking whoever was with her on a dizzying ride that was faster and brighter and more intense than anything else around.

Her name was Nadine and she grew up in Detroit. Her mother was a teacher; her father a real estate broker. We met at U-M after word spread around campus that she had set the curve on a philosophy test. If she could do it, I thought, then perhaps I could, too.

We remained friends until she committed suicide after trying and discarding a series of careers. She never thought she was good enough; I always thought she was as finely faceted as a perfect diamond. Over the years she never became involved in things like dressing for success or networking or making a conscious effort to take time for fun, while pursuing her goals, by entering "enjoyment" on her daily schedule.

And yet when you were with her, you would laugh so loud that others would begin to stare, and you would talk through the night about some new fad or experience she was trying on at the moment. She enjoyed living, even though she chose to die.

I thought about her Friday afternoon as I returned to the office from Cobo Hall after spending a few hours at something called Strategies '85, a two-day conference designed to help women in middle-management live full and productive lives while still having fun.

Phyllis George Brown, Miss America 1971 and a CBS News co-anchor, told a roomful of people the story of her life, from small-town girl to celebrity to wife and mother.

I thought I wouldn't like Phyllis George. After all, who wants to like someone with a six-figure salary, a size 8 figure, a toothpaste smile and a millionaire husband? But I found myself enjoying her talk; I laughed with her when she described her embarrassment when her Miss America crown fell off her head just as she walking down the runaway in Atlantic City; I shivered as she described sitting by her husband's bedside for three weeks after he underwent triple bypass surgery.

Then George talked about her schedule. After all, the title of her speech, according to the program, was "Can You Have it Both Ways, Family and Career?"

She's up at 3 a.m., studies for her show until 4:45, when she is driven to the studio, where she studies some more, does a two-hour morning show and then works until 5:30.

It's not easy, she said. Her life is like walking a tightrope. But one thing she has learned is to make time for fun. Make a list of things to do and remember to schedule in fun, schedule in time to enjoy life with your family. Otherwise, she cautioned, you'll be sorry one day.

Had Nadine been there, she would have laughed out loud at the very notion of scheduling enjoyment into her life. Next, she would ask, will someone tell me to schedule in breathing and blinking, and catching the spin of the Earth on a lazy afternoon?

November 4, 1985

■

A wise bird pushes baby out of the nest

PARENTS OF THE WORLD, UNITE.

Our survival is at stake here. There is a trend in this country that threatens our mental health and our financial security unless we band together to stamp out this menace.

Young adults, who previously lived on their own, are moving back into the parental home. Other young adults who are well beyond their teenage years are refusing to leave at all.

A recent newspaper article said that about half of all adults under 25 live with a parent, and one out of 10 adults between the ages of 25 and 34 lives with a parent.

In both raw numbers and in percentages, more adult children are living at home in the 1980s than in the 1970s.

Experts blame such things as poor job prospects, high housing costs and divorces for this disturbing trend.

It works this way: Mommy and daddy drive an old car, vacation in the backyard and splurge on Gallo wine so they can send little Timmy or Tammy to college or trade school. The sacrifices are made so that Little T. can become an independent person and move away from home.

Mommy and daddy don't complain about the cost of Little T.'s education; they just scrimp and save, confident that the child who threatened almost daily to leave home someday will do just that.

Mommy and daddy smile their secret smile and know that their day is coming. No more waiting to use the phone, no more busy signals whenever you try to call home, no more cookie sales, no more sweaters that walk from your closet to your kid's floor.

Happiness is seeing your child, that perfect reflection of the love between you and your spouse, pull out a door key that doesn't match yours. Parents long for that day in the same way that a hearty band of Pilgrims must have longed for the sight of the New World hundreds of years ago.

And when that day arrives, parents tearfully bid their children farewell, shut the door and break into a chorus of, "Oh Freedom."

That has been part of the American way; it is certainly part of the

71

American dream of freedom.

Now, that freedom is being threatened. Parents must preserve the tradition of separate and independent living quarters. It is our duty, Americans.

When Little T. finally leaves home, build a brick wall across the door to his or her bedroom. If the room is on the first floor and the kid can gain access through a window, hire a cement truck and fill the entire space with concrete.

If concrete clashes with your decor, join an international crime syndicate. After you've been accepted as a member, become a government snitch and get a new identity through the government's relocation program.

If that's too drastic for you, move into a one-bedroom apartment in a security building. Give the guards a recent picture of Little T. and pay them to tell the kid that your entire floor was struck by an earthquake and disappeared.

You probably think these measures are harsh, but they're not. They fit in with Mother Nature's grand design. Mama birds push their babies out of the nest when the babies become young adults. The mama birds don't let the young adults return home when worms get scarce and hard times ruffle their feathers.

Oh no. Those wise birds turn a deaf ear to the pleas of their once-independent children. Mommy bird and daddy bird just fly off to the islands, where they spend the winter flapping their wings under a limbo pole and perching on the rim of rum cocktails.

When spring arrives, they move to a new nest, get an unlisted phone, leave no forwarding address and sing themselves silly.

If you still aren't willing to follow my advice, just remember this: Mother Nature never put an empty milk carton back into the fridge.

August 31, 1988

■

Now, collect calls are most welcome

I NEVER THOUGHT "AT&T CALLING COLLECT" WOULD BE MUSIC TO my ears.

But, then again, I'm the ninny who thought the most painful separation I could possibly experience would be going through labor. I went into the delivery room as a young thing on the sunny side of 30. When I came out, the attendants wheeled me directly to the nearest senior citizens center.

You know, since those decades in the delivery room, my world has been filled with surprises. Most have come from the funny-looking stranger who took up residence in our home 18 years ago and demanded that we adjust our lives to accommodate his needs.

Last week, after a trial separation that included a three-week stint in a summer writing program at a Midwestern college, the Seeker of Wisdom and Truth officially left for college.

My Daddy, my husband, the Seeker and I piled 18 years' worth of treasure into daddy's van and headed to Howard University in Washington, D.C.

We arrived at his dorm early Saturday and managed to avoid the crush of parents and students hauling their treasures into the building.

By noon, the kid had settled in his living space. I call it a dorm. He calls it an apartment. We have a semantic battle going here. His living unit has two sleeping rooms that accommodate a total of four people, a complete kitchen and a full bath.

We spent the next three hours shopping for odds and ends — a stopper for the sink, some liquid enamel to patch the bathroom sink, extra hangers and a heavy-duty liquid cleaner. The last item was my idea.

By early afternoon, the Seeker was suggesting that we just drop him off at his apartment. He'd take care of things. We let him out at his dorm and headed back to our hotel to rest until the four of us were to go out to dinner that evening.

About an hour before we were to pick the kid up from the dorm, he called from the apartment to ask if we'd be terribly upset if he skipped dinner and went instead with his roommate, Kevin, to an ice cream social for new students.

"I guess this means he's not going to stay in the hotel with us tonight," I said in the general direction of my husband and all those years that went so quickly.

"He'll be just fine," my husband said.

Early the next morning, we headed back to Detroit. But, before we left, we stopped by the . . . uh, apartment to take some pictures and say our good-byes.

My husband, who earlier advised our son to refrain from sighing when playing poker, put his arm around the kid's shoulder and walked a little ways off. I have no idea what they talked about. All I know is that they were laughing as they returned, and they were strolling in that distinctive manner they share: Their feet turn out when they walk.

I gave the kid a hug and told him to be good.

Then the Seeker gave my daddy a hug. Daddy, who has never been short of advice on how to raise his only grandchild, started to say something, but all he could manage was, "Remember. . . . " Daddy swallowed hard, shuffled his feet and then squeezed out a "good-bye."

We got in the van and headed north. Pulling away from the curb made my trip to the delivery room seem like a brief excursion on a spring day.

"He'll be just fine," my husband said.

"When I was his age, I was heading to Germany," my husband said, referring to his tour of duty in the Korean conflict.

Daddy likes to remind me that, when he was around the Seeker's age, he was married.

Some comfort, those two. I'm trying to get used to the idea of my son being an independent — except when it comes to money — adult, and they talk of matrimony and war.

The only one who understands how I feel is the AT&T long distance operator who announces that the kid is calling collect.

In fact, the dear woman just called. Such a lovely voice. I wonder if she's thought about cutting an album.

March 10, 1989

■

Upstart son makes point at Howard

I'LL NEVER KNOW WHAT I DID TO DESERVE THIS CHILD.

When I was a college freshman like my son, I cried over any grade lower than an A and I would have bitten off my tongue before I'd defy an adult with the power to put me out of school.

I was a quivering mass of insecurity with a pixie haircut and penny loafers.

The Seeker of Wisdom and Truth obviously didn't inherit those genes.

Tell him of a worthy cause and he'll support it. Let some authority figure make an unfair or illogical demand and he'll challenge it.

So I wasn't really shocked to learn that for three days he and about 2,000 other Howard University students in Washington, D.C., occupied the school's administration building to protest, among other things, the appointment of Republican National Committee Chairman Lee Atwater to Howard's Board of Trustees.

Atwater masterminded George Bush's presidential election campaign, which included stinging, below-the-belt television ads about a black convict who raped a white woman while he was on furlough from a Massachusetts prison.

Atwater bowed to the protesters and resigned from the board. The students stayed in the building for two days, when they won written

74

promises from the school president on such issues as curriculum, campus safety, immunity for protesters and improvements in the operation of the financial aid office.

I know all this because my child called me, collect of course, to tell me. He had just returned to his dormitory after occupying the building for three days.

"I hope you're not upset with me for disobeying you," he said.

The protest began when students, including the Seeker, briefly occupied the administration building. At that time I gave him two pieces of advice: "Don't get hurt, and stay out of the way of the police."

He never listens to me. Ever.

Students were back in the building three days later, on a Monday, and organized work details to keep the protest orderly. The Seeker spent the first day or so collecting food from local restaurants and stores. "People were bringing us food left and right. A judge in line behind us at a store gave us $20."

The Seeker spent the final days working on the security detail — or more precisely, securing the roof against a police invasion.

I do not lie.

He and a dozen or so young men who labeled themselves the "Roof Men" took turns guarding against, as it turned out, pigeons.

Actually, it was a scary detail. Earlier in the protest, Washington, D.C., police were lowered onto the roof from a helicopter in a brief attempt to rout the students. The police invasion was called off almost immediately by Mayor Marion Barry but the Roof Men, including my very own shingle, never knew for sure if the police would return.

The students finally left around 4 a.m. Thursday after meeting with civil rights leader Jesse Jackson, D.C. Congressman Walter Fauntroy and Barry. The three civil rights veterans told the students they had made history. "We're going to remember this forever, Mom," my son told me. "We made history."

When I asked my child why he hadn't bothered to call home until almost nine hours after the protest ended, he replied: "The hospital was slow."

My heart froze. "My God, what happened?" I asked, almost afraid of the answer.

My son started laughing.

"I spent all that time on the icy roof and I never fell once," he said. "Then, when it was time to leave the building, I fell on the steps and sprained my ankle."

My child. I still don't know what I did to deserve him.

I guess I just got lucky.

■

Terry taught us all
how to be unselfish

THIS IS FOR TERRY.

I never wrote about him before. Now it is time.

Terry, actually Terrence, was born 20 years ago to my dearest friend. He was a beautiful baby with eyelashes long enough to leave a shadow on his cheeks and dark brown hair that toppled into huge damp curls on his forehead. He was, as I recall, a long skinny rascal, a bundle of knobby knees and elbows.

From the moment he was born, doctors suspected that something was wrong with this beautiful boy.

Finally, when he was a couple of years old, the specialists determined he had a multitude of medical problems. He was epileptic, he had poor vision and he suffered from severe developmental disorders that kept him from talking, from walking or even from crawling on the floor.

He never learned to do any of those things. Years ago when he was attending special education classes and getting daily therapy sessions, he learned to scoot on his belly. No, he didn't scoot across the floor. At best, he could do one scoot. But that was just fine with everyone who loved him.

That one motion turned out to be the peak of his physical achievements. As he grew older and ever more handsome, he became less and less flexible. His body curved in upon itself and finally, after a year of repeated crises, Terry died.

He died just five days before Christmas. His funeral was simple: a brief sermon and a few songs from a woman whose voice was as light and as pure as sunlight when it shimmers just above water.

Terry would have enjoyed her voice. It even might have made him laugh. Terry was able to hear, and he delighted in the most simple sounds: a chair dragged across a tile floor, a whistle; the sound of a voice running up and down imaginary hills, taking him on an expedition his body could never make.

My son, the Seeker of Wisdom and Truth, learned to speak to Terry in that wonderful singsong way. Terry's sister did the same thing. So did the other children in the family. They petted him and talked to him and loved him. They also learned early to keep their fingers away from his lips because he would clamp his teeth on anything that entered his mouth.

It's funny the things you remember. Terry was what specialists would call profoundly disabled. Had he had a different mother, he might have spent years in an institution. Some 4,000 people in Michigan are born with

76

such profound limitations each year.

He had to be carried, fed, diapered and bathed all of his life. In the end, he wound up in a nursing home and finally a hospital, fed through tubes.

And yet, when I think of Terry, I think of a beautiful, joyous boy who remained our baby. He taught us how to be patient and unselfish, how to see a miracle in a smile. His mom — like thousands of other parents — didn't complain about this child. She just went about the business of working full time and caring for him at home as long as she could.

He spent his last years in a nursing home, but he wasn't forgotten or left out of family holidays.

Terry was never put in a state institution, although he could have been. When he was born in 1965, some 12,500 developmentally disabled citizens were housed in state institutions in Michigan. By the time he was 10 (and still living at home), there were 6,500 people in such places. When he died, fewer than 2,200 people lived in state institutions for the developmentally disabled.

The vast majority — 85 percent — of the former residents have been moved into the community.

"Are they better off?" a friend asked when told of the figures.

"Damned straight they are," I said.

And so are we.

April 6, 1987

■

There's still plenty to be happy about

ENOUGH, ALREADY.

Enough, for now, of troubled kids, forgetful presidents and self-seeking evangelists. Enough, for now, of teenage mothers, drug-addicted babies, budget shortfalls and demonstrations at the University of Michigan.

As I write this it is Friday afternoon and I have had my fill of gloom and doom. Enough of the "half-empty glass" theory of the world. Right now my glass is half-full, the sky is intermittently sunny and the cold weather only puts roses in my cheeks.

So there.

I feel good because I have a friend of long standing whom I can call in the middle of the night with a funny line from a book or a problem that looms even more ominous in the night's shadows.

I feel good because I have a job I love, a job I adore. When I was young and new to the world of journalism, I used to get embarrassed when people would ask me where I worked. I would stammer and mumble something about working downtown and typing. If pressed I would admit I worked as a reporter for the Free Press.

And why was I so hesitant to discuss my job?

Because I honestly believed that I would be bragging if I came out and said I got paid to interview people and write stories.

I feel good because my husband of almost 20 years still makes me giggle. I feel good because we are becoming a pleasant middle-aged couple and we get tolerant smiles from young people when we walk around holding hands. I feel good because although I would die for him, I would much rather live with him — and that's not always the case in relationships.

I feel good because my feet don't hurt.

I feel good because I don't have any broken nails today.

I feel good because I will attend in a few hours a fancy program in downtown Detroit with my favorite teacher from River Rouge High School. I have known her since I was 10 years old and I have loved her every moment I have known her. I feel good because she chose to continue being my friend through the years.

I feel good because my much younger sister, who used to be my much older sister, is alive, healthy and linked with me in a bond that transcends time and space.

I feel good because I just saw a new picture of my goddaughter's twin sons, Taylor and Thurston. They are now five months old. Thurston has stolen all of Taylor's hair.

I feel good because two people recently told me that I look like my mother. My mother died more than 20 years ago and I remember her as a beautiful and gentle woman who believed that anything is possible, if only you set your mind to it.

I feel good because someone told me something very nice today about my son, the Seeker of Wisdom and Truth. I feel good because with all the problems in the world, with all the pain, I can still find joy in the simple act of looking in his face. I also can find half my best dishes by the simple act of looking under his bed.

I feel good because I talked with my daddy today. I don't recall what we said, but I like hearing his voice.

I feel good because I found a new poem that gives wings to my heart. I feel good because I know that good kids in Detroit and elsewhere far outnumber the problem kids who occupy so much of our attention.

I feel good because each day brings a new opportunity to grow and to help someone. Each day brings a new reason to laugh at myself or to laugh with someone else. Each day brings me closer to payday.

I feel good because I know when I walk into my house I will find dirty dishes, unmade beds and a sunbeam playing in a dusty corner of my living room.

I hope you feel good, too.

■

Ironing out views on steamy subject

I HAD JUST PUT A SECOND LOAD OF CLOTHES IN THE WASH AND WAS changing the linen on the bed when Oprah Winfrey, my favorite TV personality, announced that she didn't own an iron.

I unfolded a sheet, spread it on the bed and tucked in the sides. Next I held a pillow under my chin and slipped it into an old cotton pillowcase I had ironed several weeks earlier.

As I shook the pillow down into the case, Oprah told those of us in TV land that she didn't believe in ironing.

Neither do I, I mumbled as I stuffed another pillow into another ironed case, neither do I. I also don't believe in scrubbing, cooking, darning and grocery shopping.

Oprah, I thought, we have a lot in common. The only important difference between us is the ownership of an iron. The fact that you stand to earn at least $6 million this year, according to news reports, has nothing to do with our differences.

You see, if I earned $6 million in one year, I wouldn't own an iron either — I'd own 100 of them.

I'd own an oval iron for sleeves, a miniature one for ruffles, a heavy-duty one for blue jeans, a lightweight one that never gets really hot for ironing synthetic pullovers and nylon slips, and four spares to replace the one that isn't supposed to get hot, but does, and then melts your slips and sweaters. I'd own a nifty automatic shut-off model so I would never again have to rush home to make sure I had turned off the iron. And, of course, I would have a cute little collapsible iron, preferably in pastel, suitable for travel.

Don't bother telling me that hotels and motels provide irons to guests upon request. The complete traveler does not leave home without one. I may not believe in ironing, but the iron is part of my life.

When I was a little girl, Santa brought me a toy iron for Christmas. I pressed the wrinkles out of my doll's dresses. When I got older, I was allowed to stand in the kitchen and iron cotton handkerchiefs and dish towels. Soon I graduated to tableclothes and sheets. Before I knew it, I was ironing pleats and ruffles and stand-up collars and all the items in the

79

clothes basket.

Sprinkle them with water, roll them into a tight ball for a few minutes and then, quickly, slap a dollop of spit on the iron with the tip of your finger to make sure it's hot.

Blouses, towels, shorts, sweaters, skirts, dresses. I remember stacks of freshly ironed, sweet smelling sheets on the kitchen table and a line of my mother's white uniforms hanging from the top of the door. My mother worked in a supermarket.

Back then, cashiers wore white uniforms that had to be starched so heavily that they could stand up on their own.

Really, how do you exist without an iron? What do you do if you don't own a dryer and your oven breaks?

When I was a teenager I frequently dried my socks — and other items I am too modest to mention — in the oven. We didn't own a clothes dryer, so I used the oven when something had not dried completely on the clothesline. I can't begin to count the pairs of socks I owned with oven-rack scorch marks on them.

When I couldn't wait for the oven to do its work, I could always iron my socks dry — or at least iron them until they felt dry enough to put on. You know, I probably would have missed most of my first-hour classes in high school and graduated a year late if we hadn't owned an iron.

Over the years I accidentally have branded myself with old-fashioned irons and scalded my hands with steam ones. But never have I considered throwing my iron away.

After all, I want to be ready when opportunity knocks — and the dryer and stove are on the fritz.

June 8, 1987

■

Pets have things
to teach parents

TIGER SAT IN THE UPSTAIRS HALLWAY, HER DIGNITY, LIKE HER TAIL, wrapped around her.

Barkley quivered in the bedroom doorway, waiting for permission to leave.

I, the only parent in this domestic triumvirate, sat on the edge of the bed, taking notes.

I should have taped the event with a video camera.

It started when Barkley, the newest member of our household, was awakened from his nap by the announcement that his dinner was served.

It's the kind of news that normally doesn't require repeating. The dog, all 30 pounds of him, has developed three great passions in his brief lifetime: gulping down food, chewing holes in socks and pulling toilet paper through every room of the house.

He attacks them all with equal vigor.

That's why I was puzzled by this strange behavior at the doorway.

"C'mon, Barkley, dinner's ready," someone yelled from the kitchen.

Barkley jumped to attention at the sound of his bowl being placed on the floor. His ears perked up and his tail wagged so furiously that the movement sent ripples through the rest of his body.

He dashed to the bedroom door, only to stop short, as if some invisible harness held him in check. He jumped back, turned in a circle, whined, and finally lay on the floor with his head buried in the carpet.

Then, summoning some inner strength from his feral ancestors, he charged the doorway again, only to be repelled by that invisible force.

He stood in the doorway, black eyes so filled with dismay that I, too, felt a tinge of fear.

Would the same monster that intimidated my usually fearless dog also terrorize me? Would I find myself cowering on the floor, afraid to raise my head? Would I miss the start of the "Cosby Show"? Would I be trapped in my bedroom for so long that I would waste away to a size 4 and have to buy a new wardrobe, if I were ever freed?

The last thought was enough to make me face the unknown.

I leaned over to see what manner of monster had invaded my home and prevented my canine garbage disposal from eating his dinner.

And what did I see?

Tiger.

There, sitting in the hallway, was none other than our 10-year-old green-eyed bit of feline fluff who weighs no more than 8 pounds and stands about a hand high.

Tiger Watson had fixed poor Barkley with a stare and refused to allow him passage.

Every time the poor doggy tried to get by, Tiger hissed and jabbed at him with her left paw. She didn't need to hit him. A menacing swat was enough to keep him in line.

The fact that Barkley outweighed Tiger by a good 25 pounds didn't matter. The dog cowered in front of that tiny cat.

How did this happen?

Well, Tiger set down rigid rules of behavior the first day Barkley entered our home. The dog, who then was barely half Tiger's size, was not allowed to bump her with his nose, chase her, eat her food or walk past her without her permission.

All infractions were punished with a quick and sure swat across the nose. Tiger did not waver. She was consistent in her discipline. Tiger never bullied the dog nor bloodied his nose. She didn't have to. The early training she gave Barkley stayed with him. He followed her rules.

Over time, of course, Barkley grew bigger than Tiger. But Barkley never dared to call her bluff, even though he could knock her across the room with a flick of his tail.

All of which goes to prove that old cats can teach parents new tricks.

August 25, 1989

■

The long good-bye was just too short

AS FAR AS I WAS CONCERNED, MY KID COULDN'T GET OUT OF THE house fast enough.

All summer long, the Seeker of Wisdom and Truth had sprinkled hamburger wrappers and crumpled fast food bags around the den like trendy accent pieces. When an unexpected guest popped up at the door, I told her that the bags and papers were part of the decor.

"Oh, you haven't read about biodegradable art? It's the very latest thing," I lied. "A blending of aesthetics and ecology, and it only takes a second to rearrange.

"That Hardee's bag peeking out from underneath the couch is one of my favorites. It has a certain . . . ah . . . charming wrinkle to it, don't you agree?" I asked. Then I uncoiled a smile that threatened to strike my guest dead if she didn't drop the subject.

Then there was the trail of dirty socks and clean towels that marked a path from the bathroom to the kid's bedroom. No sock was discarded until it could stand up on its own. No towel ever knew more than a dewy kiss of water.

"What are you doing? Practicing for a lead role in Hansel and Gretel?" I cackled. "I promise you. You won't get lost going from the shower to your room. Just follow the sound of your radio. That's what the astronauts do when they're ready to land."

The Seeker didn't get the part in Hansel and Gretel, but I got a call about playing the witch. I had to turn it down. The timing was all wrong.

I was busy getting the kid ready to go back to college so my home could return to normal.

I had to wash, shop, drop off clothes at the tailor's and try to reunite a basketful of socks that had lost their mates. My days were filled with his leaving.

82

"Do you have enough pots and pans for your kitchen?" I asked.

"Yeah, mom, I'm all set," he said. "I don't need anything else."

"Good, then take these saucepans, too."

If it wasn't one thing, it was another. Like groceries. He said he had finished his shopping, but I knew better. No way was I going to let him stretch his stay by claiming he needed an extra day to buy more food. I spent hours roaming the aisles of the supermarket, a shopping cart at each hand.

"Are you sure you have enough food?" I asked the Seeker. I had to stand on my toes to see him over the mountain of grocery bags in the kitchen.

"Yeah, mom, I'm all set," he said. "I couldn't carry anything else."

"Good, then I'll just run to the store first thing in the morning and pick up a few more things."

The final step was packing. Every morning during his last week at home, I banged two suitcases together to wake him up.

By then, I wanted the kid out of the house so badly that even our dog, who sleeps on the foot of the kid's bed, sensed something was up. On the morning of the Seeker's last full day at home — he was scheduled to leave the following afternoon — that ungrateful four-legged beast that I rescued from the Humane Society had the nerve to bark at me when I entered my son's room.

But that didn't stop me from banging that luggage. Summer was over; time was up.

I knew that if I didn't get my son out of the house and back to school, I'd spend the rest of my days in misery.

"Smell? What smell?" I've had to ask visitors whose eyes would water as the pungent odor of gym shoe assailed them at the front door.

"Why that's just the latest fragrance out of Paris," I'd coo. "I wouldn't expect you to recognize it. After all, it's only available to a very select and discerning group of people.

"The name? Eau d'Adidas, what else?"

If the kid hadn't left, I don't think I could have kept the deception going. I hate lying. I'm just not any good at it.

That's why I stood in the driveway for 30 minutes after the kid finally took off for school yesterday afternoon. So what if it looked as if I were waving good-bye to a piece of my soul. I was just making sure he had a good tail wind.

July 23, 1987

■

Urban knight came
to riot reporter's rescue

*On July 23, 1967, Susan Watson was a young reporter at the Free Press
working on general assignment. Like the rest of the reporting staff that week —
regardless of age, experience or gender — her assignment was the riot. But unlike
her colleagues on the city desk, she found love amid the flames.*

TODAY MARKS THE 20TH ANNIVERSARY OF THE 1967 RIOT — AN
event that was, in an historical sense, more of a hiccup than a convulsion.

It flamed up, burned brightly and died down. The riot captured our
attention and made us aware of problems that were unsolved then and
remain unsolved now. But it didn't change the course of history for this
city or this nation. How could it?

Detroit's slide from prosperity to poverty began years before July 23,
1967; the decline continues today.

Still, I guess, for those of us who lived through that time, the riot made
a difference. It altered the texture — if not the course — of our lives.

Monday, July 24, the second full day of the riot.

Fires were burning and gunfire punctuated conversations across much
of the city. My editor sent me to the 10th Police Precinct in the heart of
the riot area to record, minute by minute, the events of the day.

Fat chance. The cops had no time for me. They were too busy booking
prisoners, going on runs and trying to answer questions from citizens.

So, I sat in a corner taking meaningless notes and trying to look busy. I
kept calling the office to see if I could leave, but the answer was always the
same: "Stay a little longer." I stayed, hour after hour, sitting there
watching people come and go. By the time my editor gave me permission
to leave, the sun had gone down for the count.

Local police officers and nervous National Guard troops patrolled the
streets to enforce the dusk-to-dawn curfew. I had been dropped off at the
precinct house by another reporter, and so I didn't have a car to get home.
I had enough money on me to catch a cab, but I couldn't find a cabbie
willing to turn a fare in the middle of a riot zone.

I was stranded. And so I did what any stranded single woman would do:
I called one of the two men I was dating and asked him to drive me home to
River Rouge. In the middle of the night. Through the police barricades.
After curfew.

Friend No. 1, the friend of longer standing, commiserated with me and
then, wisely, told me to stay at the cop house until morning. "It's the
safest place to be," he said before hanging up.

But I wanted to go home. So I called Friend No. 2, the friend of more recent standing.

"I'll be right there," he said. And he was. He pulled up about 30 minutes later, and then he drove me home. To River Rouge. In the middle of the night. Through the barricades. After curfew. He moved about the streets with relative safety from police because, as a member of U.S. Rep. John Conyer's staff, he was trying to help restore order.

A sane person never would have ventured into that night just to take me 15 miles to River Rouge. Those actions indicated a clear disregard for common sense and logic. Friend No. 1 gave me the right advice; Friend No. 2 acted the fool. He fancied himself an urban knight riding to my rescue in a 1966 Plymouth.

The riot finally ended. That fall, I went off to graduate school in Washington, D.C., leaving Friends 1 and 2 back in Detroit. I spent a lot of time sitting in front of an unopened textbook, thinking about my future, what I wanted to do with my life.

I thought I had put the riot out of my mind, but I guess I hadn't.

Come December, I returned home for the holidays. Two days after Christmas, I put on a white satin wedding dress — five inches above the knee — and walked down a makeshift aisle in my father's living room. My friend stood at the altar.

His 1966 Plymouth was parked out front.

May 20, 1988

■

If trash can talk, I'm in big trouble

FIRST IT WAS MY SIGN, NOW IT'S MY TRASH BAG.

The U.S. Supreme Court, in its continuing effort to unravel the sweet and legal mysteries of life, has decided that my curbside trash bag is fair game for any Tom, Dick or Private Eye who happens by on Monday morning.

My neighbors can find out that I can't keep up with the Watsons, not to mention the Joneses. Strangers can determine the state of my health, finances and emotions without even knowing my sign. And, my local cop can search for evidence linking me to some crime.

The fact that every dog, raccoon and squirrel has exercised this dubious privilege for years without damaging my right to privacy does little to ease my fears.

Dogs wag their tails, not their tongues. Raccoons don't gossip and squirrels, who bury 200 million nuts just so they can accidentally stumble across one in the winter, can't remember what they read from one

85

garbage bag to the next.

But two-legged foragers give me the willies.

As Supreme Court Justice William Brennan wrote in a dissenting opinion, "A search of trash, like a search of the bedroom, can relate intimate details about sexual practices, health and personal hygiene . . . financial and professional status, political affiliations and inclinations, private thoughts, personal relations and romantic interests."

Now, your trash may be more discreet than mine or, obviously, Justice Brennan's. If so, consider yourself lucky.

My leavings make the trash bag vibrate with tales of budgetary and dietary indiscretion. My discards tell more about my past and my future than my astrological sign ever could.

Why, just last week, honey, I had to put my trash in separate bags to keep the noise level down. You wouldn't believe what those little scraps were gossiping about.

"She says she's a size 8, but she's really a 12, heading for a 14," sneered the label that had just been snipped from a new dress.

"No wonder," crinkled the candy bar wrapper hidden inside the empty milk carton. "She hid in the closet and ate that candy so fast I thought she was going to eat me, too."

"C'mon, she's trying to do better," wept the half-empty bag of popcorn that was soaked with water. "She ate only half of me, and then she stood in front of the kitchen sink and doused me with water until I was soggy mess of carbohydrates, unpalatable even to her indiscriminating taste buds."

"She's probably pigging out because of . . . ahem . . . personal problems," whispered the copy of Cosmopolitan magazine. "Wait until you see the answers she gave on this month's connubial bliss quiz."

"It's either that, or the overdue notice from the gas company," said the envelope that bore the bad tidings from MichCon.

"She's got the money to pay; she's just careless," apologized the new paperback that got tossed in the trash amid a stack of old newspapers. "I never did get a chance to tell her how I ended."

"Careless, my eye. She's got every penny of her income already figured out through July 1, 1999. She needs the money to pay for all those doodads she buys," gossiped the scrap of paper that carried the sad tale of my finances. "Besides that, she's so busy hustling bucks that she can't even use the junk she's got."

"I am not junk and I resent your referring to me as such," huffed the warranty for the hand-held remote control TV tuner that also opens the garage door, flicks on the lights, starts the lawn sprinkler, sets off the burglar alarm, turns off the iron. . . .

"Would you guys just cut out the quibbling?" pleaded the ragged pieces of the friendly reminder that my insurance rates will go up again this year. "I'm trying to pull myself together here."

And on it goes.

You see, he who steals my purse steals trash, but he who filches my trash robs me of that sacred mirror that reflects the very core of my being: a chocolate-coated dollar sign.

■

Stripper reveals
TV's bottom line

I WAS GETTING READY TO DASH OUT OF THE HOUSE THE OTHER morning when I caught a glimpse of the opening segment of "Geraldo." OK, OK, I should have been out ministering to the sick and poor but I'm Mother Watson, not Teresa.

Anyway, because I was watching television, I now have the answer to the electronic mystery of the decade: What kinds of topics, if any, does "Geraldo" refuse to cover?

Hold your horses. First let me tell you about the episode that launched me on this investigation. I looked at the TV screen and saw someone spraying mounds of shaving cream all over the naked body of an attractive young woman, who, as it turned out, was a stripper or erotic dancer.

The next thing I knew, the woman was tippy toeing across a stage, arms gracefully waving while she did a little ballet, accompanied by classical music and hundreds of bubbles.

Then she danced over to a chair, propped one leg on the seat, picked up a straight-edged razor and proceeded to slowly shave long swaths of cream from the inside and outside of her leg and thigh — all to music, of course.

Next, she took a big sponge from a bowl of water, faced the camera and held the sponge in both hands over her head, ready to rinse away her last shield against indecent exposure.

That's when Geraldo rushed on stage and covered her with his jacket.

Mercy me, the sacrifices that poor man has made in the interest of TV journalism. His nose was broken when a fight erupted on one show. He bared his all — or almost his all — during a segment on nudism. And then, he ruined a perfectly good jacket by wrapping it around the shaving cream lady.

Geraldo described the woman as a lesbian erotic dancer. He said the show would explore sexual entertainment for lesbians. At least that's what I think he said. I was so shocked by the razor I couldn't swear to anything.

Now, this column is not about sexual preference. I don't care if the dancer was straight or gay, male or female, black or white, Protestant or Jewish. What she did with that razor was just plain weird. So weird that I called the show and asked Geraldo's spokesman if there is a topic Geraldo wouldn't cover — or uncover.

"There are a number of topics we don't do on the show," said spokesman Jeff Erdel. "Cooking. UFOs. Generally speaking the best reason for not doing a piece for us is that it will be boring. Or it's been on before or there's no new angle."

You won't see pieces on the deficit. "Geraldo" isn't trying to be a network news broadcast, Erdel said.

That wasn't what I meant. I wanted to know what kinds of ideas or suggestions were discarded because they were unsuitable; you know, tasteless. Erdel promised to call back.

As it turns out, the "Geraldo" folks killed an interview with former Washington, D.C., lobbyist Paula Parkinson, who once posed for a Playboy pictorial on Beauty and Bureaucracy.

During the taping of the "Geraldo" interview, Parkinson "made a number of accusations of a sexual nature against well-known politicans, some in office right now," Erdel said.

The show didn't run because it was potentially slanderous and defamatory. In other words, it could have cost them a bundle in court.

Interesting, but not the answer I'd sought. After all, I had seen the shaving cream lady. I wanted to know the limits beyond which Geraldo would not go.

The answer?

Dogs and dead people.

Erdel said they draw the line at "extremely aberrant sexual behavior. We wouldn't do a show on bestiality or necrophilia."

Thank heaven for that. I don't think I could survive Geraldo looking into the camera and saying in his inimitable style: "They called it puppy love. Today, on 'Geraldo.'"

June 9, 1989

■

Adoring siblings
sometimes bicker

WHENEVER MY SON, THE SEEKER OF WISDOM AND TRUTH, TRIES TO make me feel guilty for denying him a little brother or sister, I tell him about his Aunt Jan. The story usually ends his complaining, on that subject at least, for another six months.

Aunt Jan is my sister. She used to be my older sister; now she's my younger one. Back in the old days before my age leapfrogged over hers, she used to take care of me while our mother was at work.

She was around 15, raging through adolescence, and I was pushing 10. She was in high school, River Rouge High School, to be exact. I was in Miss Wright's fifth-grade class, giggling in my history book when one of the boys got paddled for acting up.

The rules around my house were simple: Jan was the big sister and I had to do whatever she told me to do until our mother got home.

In the summer, Jan would send me to Mr. Saulsberry's store to buy breakfast every morning: a bottle of Pepsi and a few pieces of Canadian bacon. We had cereal and milk around the house, but who wanted cornflakes and juice when you could have a Pepsi and a fried ham sandwich with the ham slightly burned, please?

Then she'd comb my hair and put it in pigtails and send me outside to play.

Exactly 10 minutes before Mommy walked in the door, Jan would orchestrate the fastest cleanup in history: wash the dishes and put them away, make the beds, pick up the papers off the living room floor, run the vacuum over the carpet and plop down on the sofa just as the knob turned on the front door.

As sisters go, she wasn't a particularly harsh taskmaster. To tell the truth, she was too busy being 15 to pay that much attention to me. Her life revolved around angora sweaters, Peter Pan collars, boys and going roller skating once a week.

How did I repay her kindness?

In typical 10-year-old fashion. I seized every opportunity to get her in trouble. I eavesdropped on her phone conversations and then dumped my illegally gained information in my mother's lap.

When Jan's girlfriends came to visit, they would barricade themselves in our bedroom behind a locked door and a wall of giggles. I'd scrunch up against that door and try to catch bits of information that I would use against her.

When she started smoking cigarettes on the sly, I felt duty bound to go through her coat pockets each day, searching for signs of her sinful ways. The best thing to find was a crumpled pack of Kools, but any incriminating evidence would do: a cigarette butt, a pinch of tobacco, a book of matches.

Then I'd tell Mommy: "Jan's been smoking again," and the house would rock with my sister's denials and my mother's threats which, incidentally, streamed through a blue-gray screen of Mommy's cigarette smoke.

"It's a wonder you survived," my son invariably says. "I'm surprised Aunt Jan even speaks to you at all."

I guess I'm surprised, too. I was a terrible tattling tyrant.

Some folks probably thought, with good cause, that I hated my big sister. But, to tell you the truth, I adored her. I thought she was perfect, or as close to perfect as anyone living in River Rouge would ever be. And, because I knew she would always be prettier and smarter than I, I was determined to narrow the gap between us by any means necessary.

Miracles happen. The gap did indeed narrow, but in ways I never dreamed possible.

On my last birthday — when I reached an age that still beckons on my now-much younger sister's horizon — she invited me over for breakfast. In addition to juice, homemade biscuits and eggs scrambled to perfection, she fixed a plate of Canadian bacon — slightly burned around the edges.

"This is just the way you used to like it when we were kids," she said. "We had so much fun back then."

I smiled and sent up two silent prayers of thanksgiving: one for my much younger sister and one for the fact that my son had decided to pass on breakfast.

October 23, 1989

■

With age, forgetting how to hurry up

YEARS AGO, WHEN I WAS YOUNG AND DINOSAURS ROAMED THE Earth, I used to dart from task to task like a kitten chasing a string. I was a focused, taut, fast-moving young thing, a perfect blend of strong legs and quick mind.

Give me a chore, I pounced on it. Tell me to fetch something from another part of the house, and I skipped from room to room carrying out my mission. If I needed something from an upper floor, I took the stairs two at a time.

My personal motto was simple and straightforward: If it's worth being done, it's worth doing quickly.

Those were the good old days. I knew that, as long as my legs held out, I could finish any chore in a flash. Old folks, I secretly believed, walked slowly because they were old.

Then I hit my mid-20s. Strange things began to happen.

I'd open the refrigerator and find a box of salt, a can of black pepper or an empty coffee cup inside. I hadn't shoved them in the fridge because unexpected company showed up at the door. I use the dishwasher for that.

I also can't say I was simply too tired to carry the things to the pantry.

90

After all, that pantry is where I'd find the butter dish most of the time.

No, it wasn't physical. I still moved as fast as the wind. It was just that the wind was blowing me in random directions. "Just too many things on my mind," I told myself.

When these little quirks were confined to the privacy of my home, it made life a little difficult, but we managed. I convinced my son that it was fun to have a treasure hunt in the kitchen before starting dinner each night.

But, by the time I reached my 30s, I faced a new problem. I still was able to run across the room in no time flat. But when I got where I was going, I couldn't remember why I was there.

And, to make matters worse, it happened in public.

It was so embarrassing.

I'd run across the street to the convenience store to pick up something I needed right then. The anatomical equivalent of automatic pilot propelled me safely across two lanes of busy traffic. A patterned behavioral response made me open the door.

But, once inside the store, I'd go blank. For a few numbing seconds, I couldn't remember what I wanted, what I had been in such a hurry to get. Fortunately, the reason always popped into my head just as the proprietor was glancing toward the "No loitering" sign over the cash register.

When I entered my late 30s, things got even more complicated.

I'd be rushing someplace, and suddenly, en route, I'd realize I had no idea where I was going. It wasn't merely a matter of getting there and then forgetting; it was forgetting before I got there.

Take what started happening in elevators, for example. When heading to another floor, I could still yell "Hold it!" and bolt into a crowded car before the doors closed. But when I got inside, I'd stare at those little buttons on the control panel and wonder, often out loud, where I was supposed to be going.

"I'd forget my head if it weren't glued on," I'd laugh. Some folks would join in; others would edge nervously toward the back of the elevator as if I carried some contagious disease.

That forgetfulness lasted only a matter of seconds before I could push the right button and exit on the appropriate floor. Then I'd head full tilt toward my destination. Once there, of course, I'd go blank again.

Well, after decades of being plagued by stop-and-go memory, I entered my 40s. These days, I find myself moving more like a cat lazing in the sun than a kitten pouncing after a string.

My legs no longer bother to respond when words like "run, dash, pounce, hurry and hold it!" telegraph urgent messages their way.

Flabby muscles and wheezing lungs have nothing to do with it.

My change in behavior is due to a new personal motto. To wit: If it's worth going after, take your time. That way, when you finally reach your destination, you just might remember why you're there.

■

Life has exceeded the years of dreams

THIS IS A STORY ABOUT DANDELIONS AND DAYDREAMS. IT'S FOR MY husband, who just had a birthday.

Once upon a time in a tiny factory town on the edge of Detroit, a pigtailed little girl who was more grasshopper than gazelle used to sit on her front porch and daydream about the future.

"I wonder what I'll be like when I'm all grown up," she would ask — softly, of course, so no one would hear and think her a bit odd for talking to herself.

"I wonder if I'll ever get married and who the person will be? What is he doing at this second? Have I seen him on the little connector bus that runs from my neighborhood to the main bus line? Would I like him if I saw him? Would he like me?"

The little girl with braids that always came undone didn't spend all of her time daydreaming, of course. Sometimes she stared at clouds and made them disappear. Other times she picked bouquets of dandelions from the alley behind her house and gave them to her neighbor, who rewarded her with a glass of milk and a piece of cake.

Still other times, the little girl would scrape her knees playing jacks on the sidewalk or spend an entire afternoon in the public library, reading "adult section" books that the librarians wouldn't let her take home.

The little girl grew older and traded pigtails for ponytails.

She lost the ability to make clouds disappear on a long, hot afternoon and she stopped picking dandelions out of the alley. But she still was more grasshopper than gazelle and the daydreams remained with her.

"I'm wonder if I'll ever go out on dates," she would sigh. "I'm too skinny and too tall and my feet are too long and I've never had curves in the right places, or any place at all."

The little girl, who actually was a teenager by now, had one great passionate romance. Unfortunately, it existed only in her dreams. She fell in love with a handsome upperclassman who barely acknowledged her existence. At the end of every class, she would bolt out the door and run to his classroom so she could follow him down the hall, walking in his

92

footsteps. She took cuts at the drinking fountain so she could stand behind him and drink from the fountain he had just used. She obviously had spent too much time reading paperback novels.

After high school and college, the little girl became a career woman and discovered that her attempts at loving never quite matched the daydreams. "Is there someone special for me?" she wondered.

Then, one day at a news conference, she happened to meet a most ordinary man. He called her at work the next day and he called her at home that evening. The dinner she was cooking (a hard-boiled egg) exploded while they talked. "What's that?" he asked, startled by the loud noise. "An egg," she explained matter-of-factly. "It burst."

He never asked her to fix dinner and she, of course, never volunteered. Instead, they went to movies and parties and spent hours talking and visiting friends. Once, during the 1967 Detroit riots, he drove through police barricades in the middle of the night to pick her up and drive her home.

Pretty soon the daydreams stopped. They were replaced by wedding bells and baby showers, monthly bills and parent-teacher conferences, arguments and private jokes, and shoulders to lean on or to love on.

And the lady who started off in pigtails wasn't even aware that the daydreams had ended. In fact, she was so busy living and loving that she didn't miss them at all. She also was so busy working she forgot to get her husband a birthday card, so this will have to do.

Happy birthday, kid. Here's to happily ever after.

3

KIDS
CRIME AND
BEASTMASTERS

A battler, a starry smile,
a reason to mourn

SAMUELETTA VINES AND HER FIVE KIDS HAD POSED FOR a family portrait in the living room of their apartment. The baby, Craig, 6, rested his head against her shoulder; Timothy, Marie and T'pring stood behind her, and Charles, the oldest, sat in the foreground with his Tigers cap cocked forward.

Everyone was smiling but Samueletta Vines' smile was special, like a spray of stars. She was, she told a reporter, just entering her "early golden years," when she could come and go more freely because the youngest child was in school.

With hard work and a little more luck, she could study tailoring, get a job, get off welfare and move the family into their own home.

It was all possible. You could see it in her smile.

She was 34 and had spent more than half her life taking care of youngsters, the first of whom was born when she was a 15-year-old ninth-grade dropout. Over the years, she grew kids and she grew plants and she grew laughter.

"She was the type of person if something was wrong, she could sense it," said Kathryn Evans, a friend and former neighbor. "She left some of herself with you. She opened my eyes to lots of things I never considered before . . . sewing and plants and walking. . . . She even had me jogging one day."

Samueletta Vines was always doing something, Evans remembered. Raising the kids, tending the plants that filled her apartment, whooping it up like a child during a family water fight, working out at the gym, pushing and strengthening her body until her muscles were lean and hard.

Her golden years were starting.

But then, Vines hurt her knee while working out. The pain wouldn't go away. She said it was a virus, Evans recalled, and told the kids there was nothing to worry about.

They believed her. After all, she had raised the family on her own and never stopped pushing them to make something of themselves, to stay off welfare, to compete and to succeed.

A few months went by and 14-year-old Tim told her he wanted to participate in a downtown run on behalf of a neighborhood youngster who had brain cancer. Vines helped him fill out the entry form, paid his entry fee and bought him a running outfit. Tim finished the race and gave his trophy to the neighbor boy.

When he told his mom he wanted to run a second race, this time on behalf of a sick youngster he befriended at the first race, she again helped him and encouraged him.

All the while she kept telling everyone she was fine. But Tim said the kids noticed she was losing weight and getting weaker. Finally, she told them she had cancer, her second bout with the disease. About five years earlier, she had had a double mastectomy. This time, Evans said, the cancer was in Vines' liver.

"She was strong about it," Tim said. "She knew it was just a matter of time. She knew long before she told us."

Two months later, Samueletta Vines died. But the children of her golden years, who went to live with friends and relatives, kept her smile and her spirit alive.

December 3, 1984

■

Little girl,
you shouldn't be there

TO: THE YOUNG LADY WALKING ALONE, EXCEPT FOR A STUFFED teddy bear, on the Edsel Ford Freeway at 9 p.m. Thursday night, just east of Gratiot.

From: The woman who pulled up beside you.

Re: Why I scolded you.

You, whatever your name is, probably won't read this and, if you do, you'll probably just write me off as another adult who has forgotten what it means to be young.

Maybe so, kid. But I haven't forgotten you. How could I? I was heading home from a friend's house on the east side when I noticed you walking along the side of the road, a thin young blonde woman wearing high heels and black jacket and black skirt. I thought your car had stalled and you were going for help. As the traffic sped by, I began to think how terrified I would be if I were stranded on the Ford at night.

So I got off the freeway and doubled back. To tell the truth I don't know if I would have been disappointed or relieved if I hadn't come across you again. But there you were, still wobbling along on those high heels.

I pulled over, tooted the horn and, within a few seconds, looked into the face of a child, a child with bleached blonde hair, too much makeup and eyes that spoke more poignantly than she ever could. I looked into the face of a child who was clutching a tattered brown teddy bear to her chest.

I wasn't ready for you, little girl. I wasn't ready for a kid with a voice like a question mark, a kid who said she had hitchhiked down from Port Huron and was heading for East Warren and Helen. I wasn't prepared to deal with a youngster who said she was 18 but looked even younger.

I was afraid for you and afraid of you. I was afraid to leave you wandering along the roadside and I was afraid to let you inside my car. I didn't know if you had a gun or a friend who was waiting just out of sight. All I knew was that I couldn't leave you there.

That's why I scolded you, kid; that's why I said you were old enough to know better than to go wandering around the roads at night. That's why I told you that you made me feel like your mother and I didn't like it. And that's why I threw my purse in the backseat and was getting ready to open the door when a tow truck pulled up behind us. When one of the men inside asked if we were all right and then reluctantly offered you a ride, I thanked him and then wrote down the company name on the side of the truck just in case.

All day I've been wondering if you're safe; all day I've been troubled about being afraid to help you.

You won't read this, little girl, but I needed to say it anyway.

To: The guys in the truck.

From: The lady by the side of the road.

Thanks for stopping; thanks for getting me off the hook.

To: My husband.

From: The lady who did exactly what you told her never to do, the lady who stopped on the highway at night for a stranger.

I'm glad I stopped but I don't know if I'll do it again. The fear was too raw, the responsibility too overwhelming.

To: My son who was washing dishes at the rate of one plate an hour when I walked in the house, my son whose room could be declared a disaster area; my son who never met a meal he didn't like.

From: Your mom, who knows that somewhere there's someone who loves the little blonde girl as much as I love you.

Go clean your room and do your homework . . . and give me a hug.

October 30, 1985

■

Shotgun pellets
are her souvenir

I HAD NEVER SEEN WHAT A SHOTGUN CAN DO TO A PERSON. IN truth, I had never given the matter much thought.

Everything I knew about shotguns came from Saturday matinees at the old Lancaster Theater in River Rouge. A farmer would aim a shotgun at an intruder and fill his behind with pellets. The intruder would jump into the air, grab his rear and head for the hills.

Shannon didn't jump into the air. The force of the blast knocked her forward, leaving her unable to move. Someone carried her down from the top row of the bleachers, where she had been watching a football game. Someone else took her to the hospital.

Her friends later told her they heard three shotgun blasts. She can't remember.

Her friends told her the assailants drove into the Murray-Wright High School parking lot and fired into the stands, where hundreds of students were watching a homecoming football game. Shannon didn't see anything.

She was, she said, concentrating on the game.

Shannon, a sophomore at Murray-Wright, was one of six youngsters wounded that afternoon. An argument at a pep rally may have led to the shooting.

Two victims, including Shannon, were hospitalized overnight; a third suffered a fractured skull and also has now been released from the hospital.

Seventy-two pellets from a shotgun tore into Shannon's jeans and bit into her legs from her ankles to her thighs. Some of the pellets nicked her, others slammed inside.

I know there are 72 pellet wounds because Shannon's mother counted them, one by one, when the child came home from the hospital. Upper thigh, back of the knee, calf, ankle, side of the leg, front of the leg. The child's legs are covered with tiny scabs.

If you run your hand over the area just below her left knee, you can feel pellets protruding against the skin, hard little lumps on a child who wears red barrettes on the ends of her braids. Shannon's legs were hurting, and she was moving with the aid of a walker, holding one leg slightly bent to keep her weight off of it.

Shannon's mother said the youngster wanted to talk about what had happened. When I arrived at their home, the mother gave me a statement Shannon had written, a statement saying most kids are good and only a few cause problems. The mother, a secretary, had typed it.

Shannon's mother is into positive thinking; Shannon's 19-year-old sister is into rage. Most kids, the mother said, don't carry guns and don't cause problems. "This is not an everyday situation," the mother continued. "If it were, Shannon would be afraid to return to school, and she's not."

Shannon's older sister cannot let the incident rest. She picks at it like a scab. "She's only 15 years old," she rages.

How dare they do this to her?

While the conversation goes back and forth, Shannon studies her reflection in the dining room mirror. Her sister and mother are caught there too, their drama played out in pantomime.

Every now and then, Shannon turns her head and laughs at her sister's rage or her mother's determination to be positive. She laughs and the laughter sounds so much like sobbing that you stare at her eyes, expecting tears.

"I don't know what to think," she says. "My sister is saying negative stuff, my mother is saying positive stuff." She just wants to be left alone.

After all, the child says matter-of-factly, the gunman wasn't after her; he was after someone else. All she has to do, she says, is stay away from trouble and she'll be fine. Nobody wanted to hurt her. It wasn't her fault. She hadn't done anything wrong.

"If you write something about this, please make it positive," the mother repeats. Make it positive but don't identify us in the paper, she says. You never know what some people might do.

January 21, 1987

■

A nameless group fights senseless spree

THE GROUP WITHOUT A NAME HAS TAKEN ON THE PROBLEM THAT laughs at solutions.

I like that. The notion of an unnamed community group's coming together to try to tackle the seemingly uncontrollable epidemic of teenage shootings and killings is, in an odd way, fitting.

"We don't have time right now" to waste our energy selecting a name and electing officers for this and that, explained the Rev. Richard Randall, the minister who helps direct the group without a name.

Still, the group without a name has a specific goal — finding a way to eliminate, or at least reduce substantially, the obscene number of young people shot to death in our city.

And on Sunday, a couple hundred people — black and white, young and old, elected officials and just plain interested citizens — showed up at the Church of the New Covenant-Baptist to see just what a nameless group could do about a seemingly intransigent problem.

By the end of the meeting, the group without a name had decided to hold a memorial service on Feb. 8 to honor the 43 youngsters under the age of 17 who were shot to death in Detroit last year.

During the meeting, the group did decide to write letters to Gov. James Blanchard and local officials, asking them to proclaim the week leading up to the memorial service as a week of prayer. The group will also ask the public schools to set aside a few minutes during that week so our children still with us will be reminded of the tragedy of lost lives.

And the group wants everyone to wear a red ribbon during that week of prayer. Local churches will be asked to light a red candle during services. You could probably tie a red ribbon to your door or tack one on a tree without offending the group without a name.

Now, some folks, sophisticated in the ways of community organizing, have said that the group without a name needs more structure. It needs an agenda, maybe a staff person, a coordinator at the very least.

Well, maybe. But for now, the group is doing just fine. It has set as its immediate goal the memorial service and events leading up to it. After that, it will begin to tackle the other problems that beset us.

The group without a name is moving in small, cautious steps. But that caution shouldn't be mistaken for a lack of will. You see, the group without a name is driven by the inextinguishable power of a group of mothers whose children have been shot to death in Detroit.

There's Clementine Barfield who lost her son Derick. Vera Rucker who lost her daughter Melody. Anita Totton who lost her son Anthony.

These women — along with others who shared the same tragedy — are the driving force behind the group without a name. Their combined will can move mountains. I believe that.

They have taken the lead in this struggle. Sure, they'll make some missteps, but every new group does — even those that have a name.

At least this group is doing something.

Which reminds me. Monday night I attended a memorial for Dr. Martin Luther King Jr. Mayor Coleman Young was there. Young, who has yet to provide us with the moral leadership we need in this crisis, told the gathering that Detroiters need to get off their behinds and start attacking the problem of youth violence. The solution must begin with us, said the mayor who is still trying to get his crime plan together.

There was an echo in Cobo Hall.

I wonder if the mayor could hear his own words.

April 3, 1987

■

Here's an apology to one sorry punk

I OWE AN APOLOGY TO A YOUNG PUNK.

About two weeks ago, my son, the Seeker of Wisdom and Truth, and I went out to breakfast on a school-day morning. Since the Seeker didn't have a first-hour class that day, we decided to treat ourselves at a neighborhood restaurant.

The restaurant isn't a fancy place by a long shot. It's one of the hundreds of storefront eateries in Detroit that specialize in home cooking at reasonable prices.

If you're in a hurry, go to McDonald's. If you want homemade vegetable soup and heavy corn muffins dripping with butter, go to this place — a nice, quiet place where the sizzle of bacon on the grill competes with the rustle of newspapers being turned to the sports section. It's the kind of place that attracts working adults, shoppers, kids, students and senior citizens.

Now, in all my years of eating there, I had never eaten breakfast there on a school-day morning. Lots of Saturday brunches and summer lunches, but never an early morning cup of coffee while the kids were headed to school.

Was I in for a surprise.

The front of the restaurant was filled with youngsters carrying textbooks and papers. The kids occupied all the booths and spilled over into the aisle. They were noisy, but not rowdy.

My son and I were standing at the counter, waiting to place our order when, for some reason, the youngsters turned up their noise level full blast.

The owner asked the kids to leave. Time to get out, she said politely. You're making too much noise, time to go.

The kids stood up and headed toward the door. Then one young man said to his friends in a loud voice: "I'm always getting kicked out of some ---damn place. Every m-----f------ place I go, they ask me to leave."

The kid was no more than 14. I'm sure he didn't shave yet and he was just over 5 feet tall. Yet, he let loose a string of profanities as if it were the most normal thing in the world for him to do.

I felt as if someone had slapped me.

But I didn't say anything. Neither did the three men hunched over their food at the counter.

I didn't say one word to that rude young man, even though my first impulse was to stop him in his tracks and give him a tongue-lashing he would long remember.

"Who is your mother?" I wanted to ask. "How dare you, young man, speak that way around adults, and particularly women? You know better than that and, if your parents were here, they would beat the living daylights out of you."

But I didn't. I just watched him leave the restaurant and then I muttered something to the owner about scandalous behavior. She shrugged her shoulders and took another order.

103

I feel bad every time I remember that incident. I should have said something to that young man, but I didn't. I was afraid, pure and simple, that he might hurt me for scolding him.

Hell, I didn't know if the kid was armed. And, in all truth, I feared that, if I challenged him, he and his friends might reciprocate, and my son might wind up battling a roomful of kids to protect his mom, who couldn't mind her own business.

So I kept my mouth shut. And by doing that, I did that child — and mine — a disservice. I let him know that adults will let him get away with unacceptable behavior, that adults can be bullied and intimidated by kids. That youngster may have been testing the bounds of his adolescence. By my silence, I let him tumble over the edge. This time no one was hurt, physically. I don't know what will happen next time.

All I know is that I failed that kid. And for that, I owe him an apology, even if he is a punk.

April 20, 1987

■

Who shot Chester?
Look in the mirror

WELL, FOLKS, WE KILLED 17-YEAR-OLD CHESTER JACKSON AT Murray-Wright High School Thursday. We, not some anonymous they, shot the football player in the face. We also wounded student Damon Matthews and left a bullet lodged somewhere in his head.

A 14-year-old is in custody for the shootings, but we are responsible. We allowed a youngster not old enough to vote or to buy a drink or to get a credit card to carry a gun in school.

We allowed a 14-year-old to believe that he could walk the streets with a gun and use the weapon to settle some real or imagined grievance.

We killed Chester Jackson because we have been unwilling as men and women to come together to save our children.

We killed him because we as black people are so accustomed to being victims, so used to blaming others for our problems, that we do not get off our sorry behinds and take action. Like it or not, it's the truth.

We killed Chester Jackson because we said the teenage violence is too complicated and too widespread to control.

We killed him because we have allowed the intractable problems of racism and unemployment and drug addiction to crush our will to fight back. Of course, we must recognize the historical impact of racism on our lives. But after understanding that reality, we have to look to ourselves to change things.

No one is going to do it for us. The federal government is not going to ride to the rescue of Detroit's children. And, realistically, why should we expect someone else to worry about the deaths of black men when those deaths reduce the numbers of unemployed and underemployed Americans?

Why should someone else worry about the incarceration of so many young black men when thousands of people get their paychecks from the criminal justice system?

Why should anyone worry about us when we don't care enough about ourselves to protect our children? I'm not talking about morality. I'm talking bloody, brain-spilling reality.

Maybe we can't stop the flow of drugs into the city. Maybe we can't create decent-paying jobs.

But we can do something.

We can walk the halls and the parking lots of our schools. We can push for a tax hike to pay for the protection and nurturing our kids need. We can demand that schools and community centers stay open longer and increase their services for kids. We can lock away our guns or get rid of them. We can turn off the TV, put down our designer bags and begin to work with our young.

And we can learn to say "NO." No staying out late. No $75 status gym shoes on a kid who can't read. No hats cocked sideways. No beepers. No ropes of gold or imitation gold.

Why are we allowing so many of our black children to walk around looking like drug dealers when most of the kids are just imitating that culture?

I am sick and tired of excuses.

If Jews can pull together to teach their children about their history, why can't we? If Chaldeans can pool their resources, come into the Detroit community and work seven days a week, 12 hours a day to get a business going, why can't we? If little Vietnamese children who come to this country unable to speak English can become scholars, why can't we?

We may live in an impoverished city, but do our souls have to be impoverished too? We have a rich and proud history to sustain us. Our slave ancestors valued their children above all else.

Now, we, the sixth or seventh generations, sit by while our children are dying and while those who survive are crying for help.

That 14-year-old may have had the gun. But we, brothers and sisters, pulled the trigger.

■

Why did this death touch city's nerve

WHAT MAKES CHESTER JACKSON'S DEATH DIFFERENT FROM ALL the others?

What was it about his death that prompted Mayor Coleman Young to tell a crowd of 8,200 people that he was so "tired of kids shooting down kids" that he was ready to send police into schools to search for weapons?

What is it about the young Murray-Wright High School student's death that prompted the mayor to say that juveniles caught with guns will be thrown in "police jails" if there is not enough space for them in juvenile facilities?

This is the same mayor who has vigorously opposed gun control measures because he said the city, state and county lack adequate space to house offenders.

What is it about Jackson's death that prompted schools Superintendent Arthur Jefferson to say, after Young's speech, that the school board plans to return to court to reopen the case on the use of weapons sweeps in the schools?

School officials have been complaining for a year about procedures that require students to be notified before a weapons search is conducted. These are the same procedures, mind you, that were drawn up by the school board's attorneys and then approved by U.S. District Judge Avern Cohn. If the board didn't like the rules, why didn't it return to court before this tragedy?

Was it the moaning and groaning about the weapons searches that prompted Judge Cohn to order a review to see if those rules really were to blame for making it difficult to keep the schools safe?

What is it about Chester Jackson's death that has revved up the movers and shakers and caused them to take action?

Of course, we mourn Jackson's tragic death. But we also mourn the tragic deaths of the 43 youngsters age 16 and younger who were killed last year in Detroit. We mourn the nine other youngsters killed this year.

We mourn the death of a four-year-old boy who found a gun under a bed in his house and accidentally shot himself.

But I still want to know, why is there a moving fury over Jackson's death, but only muted sadness over the deaths of the others?

Part of the reason, I guess, is that Jackson was shot at school. He was killed in an institution we want to consider inviolable. Schools are places where we pass along our knowledge and our traditions to our young, where we prepare them for the future. Schools are the last bastions of

106

safety in an unsafe world, we think.

Schools are places with boundaries and walls. If we can't keep them safe, we cannot keep any place safe. Maybe Jackson's death is different because it shows how impotent we have become.

I want to know why Chester Jackson's death is different from all the others. We need to know because knowing will help us understand how to go about getting action on all the other deaths.

Knowing what activator button this poor child's death triggered may help sound the alarm for the other children we may lose, the children who are wounded as they walk down the street or play basketball on a neighborhood court or stand on a front porch after a party.

A youngster I have known for years was in the Murray-Wright High School cafeteria when the fatal shooting spree began. I thank God she wasn't physically wounded that day.

But the fact remains that she and all of our children could fall victim to handgun violence just as dozens already have.

And, unless we find out why Chester Jackson's death is different, we may continue to react to the other deaths with only impotent rage.

April 24, 1987

■

You can't hide gun from curious kids

YOU MAY HAVE MISSED THE MOST IMPORTANT BIT OF INFORMATION in the newspaper. I did, until someone pointed it out to me.

It was contained in the eighth paragraph of a late-edition story about plans by Detroit school officials to suspend high school classes for two days so that parents and students can attend in-school meetings about guns and parental responsibility. The meetings come in the wake of the fatal shooting of a student at Murray-Wright High School.

The paragraph in question read:

The weapon recovered at Murray-Wright was a .357-caliber handgun registered to the father of a 14-year-old ninth-grader suspected of the shootings, according to law enforcement officials, who said preliminary indications suggest no negligence by the parents. The gun apparently had been stored in a locked container, the officials said.

Look, folks. If you have a gun around the house, your child will find it and examine it.

If you are lucky, the kid will return it to its hiding place without taking it outside. But don't count on being lucky. Don't even count on being safe because you think you are a responsible gun owner.

Kids are snoops. If you have a gun in your home, your child — not someone's child — might sneak it out of the house and take it to school or to the playground or just into the backyard.

Your child — not someone else's child — might carry the gun to settle a grievance or to protect himself or herself or to gain status among friends.

If you have a gun in the house, you need to keep it broken down, unloaded and locked away in different parts of the house. Even then, there's no guarantee that your little darling — not someone else's problem child — will not find all the pieces, put them together and point the weapon at someone else's child.

If you have to have a gun around the house, pray that your luck holds out until all your kids and their kids and your friends' kids no longer rummage for forbidden treasures.

Thousands of decent, law-abiding people keep guns in their homes to protect their families. More often than not, the "family" gun will do more to destroy a family than to protect it.

The Board of Education officials will talk about gun safety and kids at two meetings. It's a talk that's long overdue. I don't know if the sessions will do any good; they certainly won't do any harm. And at the very least they will dramatize our heightened concern about kids and guns. It's a start and it should be applauded.

The talks also should be attended. Some seasoned educators and community workers already are predicting that only a handful of parents will turn out for the sessions. The ones who need to hear the message most may miss it because they are convinced that other things, like jobs or shopping or TV shows, are more important.

Well, wouldn't it be nice if the TV and radio stations announced the meeting at regular intervals over the weekend? Wouldn't it be nice if all these churches around the city urged their members to attend the meetings just as they urge members to put money into the collection plate? Wouldn't it be nice if the school system made an extraordinary effort to contact the parents of kids who are having trouble?

Wouldn't it be nice if everyone, from my boss at the Free Press to Mayor Coleman Young to the folks at the News to the operators of local stores and malls, went out of the way to urge folks to attend the meetings?

And, since I'm floating questions anyway, wouldn't it be nice if we decided to test our luck in Las Vegas instead of here at home?

■

No time for music,
guns must fall silent

THIS IS NOT THE COLUMN I INTENDED TO WRITE. I HAD DECIDED during my vacation to start the New Year on a joyously positive note — a note, actually a series of notes, so pure and clear that their sounds would carry like the music from a wind chime.

In the midst of so much tragedy and pain, I wanted to write about triumph. Maybe "triumph" is too strong a word. I wanted to write about the tiny, blink-of-an-eye, baby's smile success stories that give us the strength to carry on.

I've got the whole year to poke out my hip and my lower lip over one problem or another, I reasoned.

I even smiled as I thought about concocting a sugary little confection that would manage to fatten the lean portions of the soul.

Then I learned about Aaron.

Aaron was one of the students in a beginning newswriting class I taught last semester at Wayne State University. He was bright but tended to hold back in class. At 19, he's interested in becoming a newspaper editor. He lives in Detroit, graduated from a public high school and is a college sophomore.

Aaron and the other class members spent hours learning how to write basic news stories — obituaries, three-paragraph fillers, crime stories, speeches, interviews.

Aaron got off to a rocky start. But, by the end of the class, he was producing pretty good work.

The class was over and I had handed in the final marks when I received a letter from Aaron. It was written in the form of a newspaper story, double-spaced and with appropriate copy-editing marks. He started the first page halfway down the paper, just as I had taught him. At the end of each page, he wrote "MORE," and circled it. At the end of the final page, he typed a line of #s and circled that, indicating that he was finished.

He did everything just the way I had taught him, down to giving the story a short name or slug, as we call it.

Aaron slugged his story "close."

"At about 1:30 p.m. Tuesday afternoon, I decided to mail a package to a friend in the Army," Aaron began. He mailed the package at a post office near his home, stopped to buy a box of M&M's from a little boy at the door and then headed home.

"The snow was too deep to walk on the sidewalk, so I walked down the middle of the street. I saw a thin man, digging in his pants, coming toward me. . . . We were about to pass each other when he pulled out a gun that looked like a cannon to me. I saw it and my heart raced. All I could think about was that I was going to be another statistic."

The gunman took Aaron's money and told him to run. Aaron did just that. The gunman fired two shots. Both, thank God, missed the mark.

"I am so grateful," he wrote, "that my mother did not become like other mothers in Detroit who lost their sons and daughters. I am so glad that my sister still has someone to complain to my mother about for staying in the bathroom. I am so glad my brother still has someone to exchange cassette tapes with. I am so glad my friend in the Army will have someone to listen to her Army stories when she comes home, and I am so very glad that Christmas will not be a time that my 2-year-old nephew remembers as the time his uncle died."

Had Aaron handed this story in as a class assignment, I would have filled it with corrections and covered it with question marks.

But it wasn't an assignment. And when I finished reading Aaron's story, I cried. I cried because he was safe, and I cried because he almost became a victim of our insane love affair with handguns.

Each year handguns account for about 9,000 homicides nationwide. It is time for me to dry my eyes and to start fighting.

The sound of the wind chime will come later.

January 8, 1988

■

Bring urban crack
to suburban users

MIKE WENDLAND OF THE CHANNEL 4 I-TEAM GAVE ME THE IDEA. All of us — Detroiters and suburbanites alike — are in his debt.

Last month the I-Team ran a special investigative report on the crack cocaine business in Detroit. The series focused on a narrow slice of Detroit's east side where the sale of crack cocaine is rampant.

The I-Team, which spent several days watching drug transactions in the streets, kept a list of the license plate numbers of some 50 cars involved in those business deals.

State records revealed that 70 percent of the cars were registered to people who live outside Detroit.

Clients came from places like Mt. Clemens, Warren, Harper Woods, Sterling Heights, Roseville, St. Clair Shores, Royal Oak and Grosse Pointe.

A similar though separate bit of reporting by Free Press reporter

Darryl Fears produced similar findings. Fears spent weeks reporting on a neighborhood riddled with crack houses. Drug dealers told him that many drive into the city from the suburbs.

Well, my pets, it seems to me that this is a classic example of a consumer problem that cries out for a quick and convenient solution.

I can sympathize with that problem. After all, I live in Detroit and I know what a bother it is to have to leave the city to find a major department store or a multi-purpose, one-stop shopping mall.

Detroit was left behind by thousands of stores and businesses that darted across the city limits to satisfy the demands of suburban consumers.

That's just good business sense, some would say. And, heck, I'm not going to argue. Business follows the buck. Any entrepreneur who is smart enough to spot a trend or to identify a gap in the marketplace can get rich.

And that's why my idea is perfect. There's a gaping hole in the suburban retail market, and I know how to fix it.

Right now, hundreds or thousands of suburbanites have to drive all the way to Detroit to buy crack cocaine. That's not fair to them. That's a waste of time and gas.

The solution: Move the crack houses out to the burbs.

Detroit has an estimated 8,000 to 13,000 crack houses. If 70 percent of the customers — or even 50 percent or 30 percent of the customers — come from suburbia, then a similar percentage of the retail crack establishments should be sprinkled among the communities where the customers live.

That's only fair. Just imagine the convenience of having your very own crack house in your neighborhood. If news reports are correct, the suburbs need at least 3,000 additional crack houses to meet the needs of local consumers.

The exact number of houses in each city would depend on the results of a marketing survey, paid for, of course, by each community. After all, cities have been offering incentives to attract businesses for years. The survey would allow each city to get its fair share of cocaine retail establishments.

I can't see how anyone could object to my idea. It is a logical extension of what's been going on for years.

I'd even bet that Mayor Coleman Young and the City Council members wouldn't make a peep about the loss of a major employer in the city.

And, in time, the people who live in the neighborhoods blighted by crack cocaine sales to Detroiters and suburbanites would get used to having fewer crack cocaine outlets. In time, the neighbors would learn to accept quieter streets, less dope traffic and fewer youngsters protecting their turf with guns.

After all, we are Detroiters, and we are accustomed to doing without.

Crack house child,
what do you do?

IT WAS A QUESTION FOR WHICH THERE WAS NO SATISFACTORY answer. But I posed it, just the same.

"What was your child doing in that crack house?" I asked the woman on the other end of the line.

One answer had appeared in the paper the day before:

A 16-year-old kid was rolling drugs from an east side house. The youngster told police he had worked two months for a man who had given him crack to sell and a rifle for protection.

The thing that makes this story stand out from all the other stories about kids and crack is that this youngster killed a man who was breaking into the crack house. The kid got off on a ruling of self-defense.

Though he admitted dealing drugs, he wasn't charged because he was clean when the cops arrested him.

I didn't talk to the kid's mother to find out what he was physically doing in the crack house. That was obvious. I was trying to find out what this 16-year-old kid was doing there; how he wound up selling rocks of cocaine out of an east side house instead of going to school or working in a burger joint or running on the track team or watching TV. If you'll show me how you went wrong, I thought, you'll also show me how I can go right.

And so, with the grace of a one-eyed bull in a china shop, I asked the mother: "What was your child doing in that crack house?"

She knew the easy answer, but not the other one. "I don't know," she said, her voice tired and hollow.

"Did you know that he was selling drugs?"

She said she didn't.

"But surely you must have had some indication that something was wrong," I persisted.

"I thought he was doing something wrong," she said, "but when I asked him, he said he wasn't."

"Where did you think he was all those nights when he was gone from home?"

"He said he was spending the night with friends."

"Your son is 16 and in the ninth grade. Does he have problems in school?"

"He's not in school," she said. "He stopped going" earlier this year.

"Why didn't you make him go?"

"I tried, but I couldn't."

112

Near the end of the conversation, the woman tried to salvage a shred of dignity for the family she heads.

He knew better than to sell drugs, she said. He knew it was wrong. How did he know?

Well, not too long ago, his older brother got in trouble with drugs, the mother said. The whole family was threatened by dealers. Her words, just like her life, seemed to tumble off a cliff. They never echoed; they never hit bottom; they never bounced back, battered but wiser by the fall. They just tumbled into the void.

A month later, I got a piece of the answer I was seeking. It came at a panel discussion on kids and drugs at the Unity Temple of the Apostolic Faith in Detroit.

One of the panelists was Kenneth Danzy, an administrator of the Wayne County Youth Home. Danzy sees hundreds of kids like that 16-year-old. Most of them sell drugs for the money. Most are behind in school. Most come from single-parent homes. The kids aren't addicted to crack; they're addicted to gold chains and gym shoes, cars and wads of money.

Sometimes — far too often — that addiction spreads to parents who don't care or who refuse to admit where the extra cash comes from. All they care about is that it's there.

Danzy told me about a kid — not the one mentioned above — who needed 10 minutes to put on his gold jewelry when he was released from the Youth Home. He had rings for each finger, a watch for each arm and a chestful of gold.

His mother picked him up — in his sports car. She said she didn't know how he got the money.

"But that must be the exception," I said. "Maybe I'm naive, but surely most parents don't profit from their kids' selling drugs, do they?"

"You're naive,' he said, and his words tumbled off that same deadly cliff. Only this time, they ricocheted off the sides, bounced off the bottom and set up a chorus of echoes almost too painful to hear.

August 24, 1988

■

All that glitters need not be seen

I HAD SLIPPED INSIDE THE DINING ROOM ON THE CRANBROOK campus to escape the heat. All I was looking for was a little shade, maybe a cup of water.

Then I saw this long lanky kid, all arms and legs and knees and feet, walking toward the kitchen. He had on shorts and a T-shirt and maybe a cap, I'm not sure. He and a friend were laughing at a private joke.

I noticed the youngster because he was so tall. I could see him shooting hoops in a driveway or dunking the ball in a school gymnasium.

Then I caught a snatch of the conversation with his friend. You'll never guess what it was.

Hamlet's soliloquy. You know, the "to be, or not to be" speech.

I wish I could say I forgot about the heat for the rest of that afternoon, but that would be a lie. I did, however, feel the cool breeze of unlimited possibilities every time I thought about him.

The youngster was among some 270 mostly inner-city public school students who are participating in an educational enrichment program called Horizons — Upward Bound at the Cranbrook Educational Community in Bloomfield Hills. The program has been around for nearly a quarter of a century, providing special summer sessions and weekend classes during the school year for bright kids from less than privileged backgrounds.

The program follows the participants though four years of high school and then helps them get into some of the most prestigious colleges in the country.

I was at Cranbrook earlier this month for the end-of-summer student exhibition and awards ceremony for Upward Bound youngsters who had excelled in subjects such as English, calculus, physics and chemistry.

Program director Ben Snyder talked briefly about the values of hard work. And as he talked I thought about these special kids, who will carry with them knowledge about Shakespeare and isosceles triangles, kids who can convert Fahrenheit temperatures into Celsius and miles into meters.

How lucky they are.

They can delight forever in their invisible treasures.

Then I thought about two other kids I saw earlier that week.

The first one was standing in line in front of me at a west side store. I noticed him because of what he wore — blue jeans, a snakeskin belt and a matching snakeskin beeper case attached to the side of his belt. He wore so many gold chains around his neck that his chest appeared to have been dipped in molten gold.

He bought a pack of cigarettes, paid with a $20 bill, and then dashed out the door — young, strong and wearing his treasures for all to see.

The other young man walked into a store on Woodward where I was looking for shoes. He had on jeans, a T-shirt and gym shoes. He, too, carried a beeper. His gold chains were modest by comparison to those of the other young man.

I forget what this young man bought. All I can remember is that he pulled out a wad of money that was bigger than a fist. I can see him now,

114

peeling off those bills, one by one.

He, too, wore his treasures for all to see. He pulled them out and flaunted them, then he shoved them back in his pocket.

My husband calls these kids urban nomads. The are loaded down by the weight of their possessions. Things. Gold, beepers, designer clothes, Jeeps, lumps of money. They carry with them in their pockets, around their necks and on their bodies everything that they hold dear.

I wonder, what happens to a child when he can put a price tag on everything he values, when most of his treasures are visible? Does he begin to believe that individual worth can be measured in karats or dollars? Does he stop caring about invisible things, such as other people's feelings, community pride, decency? I don't know the answers.

All I know is that I didn't notice an ounce of gold on my friend at Cranbrook.

Still, he glittered and glistened, his invisible treasures lighting his world — and mine.

August 26, 1988

■

Ignoring evil will only help it grow

TWO GROUPS OF FOLKS ARE ABOUT TO DRIVE ME OVER THE EDGE: gun-wielding teens who are too young to enter an R-rated movie and darned fool parents who know more about the private lives of the kids on the "Cosby Show" than they know about the lives of their own children.

Our kids are killing each other at a record rate, and far too many of us parents observe the carnage like spectators at a cockfight.

We stand back, wince and try not to get any blood on our clothes. We hope our child does not get into the ring. But, when that child does fall into the trap of violence, the parent shakes his head and invariably describes the shooting, robbing, school-skipping, murdering, dope-selling youngster as "a good child." Then, in almost the same breath, that same parent professes ignorance of any illegal activities by Johnnie, Jimmie, Billie, Sue.

"I didn't know what he was doing."

"I didn't know he had a gun."

"I can't control that boy."

We have become one sorry bunch of parents. We see nothing, hear nothing and speak nothing, and we hope that our studied attempts at ignorance will keep evil from our door. We ought to be ashamed of

115

ourselves.

We have let fear and a sense of hopelessness prevent us from helping our children.

You know, fear is a funny thing. Most adults wouldn't think twice about rushing into freeway traffic to rescue a child who had wandered into harm's way.

It's a natural reflex. People risk their lives every day to rescue youngsters from hopeless situations — burning buildings and traffic accidents and oncoming cars.

But we won't take what may or may not be the same risk to save our kids from themselves.

Think about it. We accept the unacceptable from our children. How often have you asked a child, other than your own, to turn down his radio? How often have you let someone else's child know politely that m-----f----n' is not an all-purpose adjective in polite society?

Ask an adult why he or she won't confront a misbehaving youngster, and the response runs something like this: "You can't say anything to them; they might do something to you. They won't listen anyway."

I've used that excuse, too. But it's just not good enough anymore.

We have to stop being afraid to talk to our children. We have to remind them, as others reminded us, of what is right and wrong, what is acceptable behavior and what isn't.

I don't think it's as difficult or daring as it sounds.

On the streets, we have to look a child in the eye and say, "Good morning, young man." We have to say, "I beg your pardon, young lady" when a kid uses gutter language. We have to have the courage to get in their business and to stay on their case, to let them know we care.

And what, you may ask, has launched me on this latest tear?

A parent, what else?

The mother of a 16-year-old accused in the shooting death of a 14-year-old on a city bus reportedly said she was unaware her child had a gun. But then she added: "I don't know where they get them but they all have them, don't they?"

Lord, save us all. Everyone, quick, run out into the street and scream at the top of your lungs: All children do not carry guns! Some do, but most of the approximately 200,000 young people in Detroit between the ages of eight and 18 do not walk around with revolvers tucked in their waistbands or purses.

It's not true that all kids carry guns. But as long as adults shrug their shoulders and tacitly accept such obscenely false conclusions — and as long as we pass along those false conclusions to our children — we will be in trouble.

As long as we allow ourselves to be made impotent by fear and hopelessness, we will continue to have tragedies like the one on that city

116

bus.

You see, the 16-year-old said he shot the other youngster because he thought the 14-year-old was going to pull a gun.

After all, everyone has them, right?

January 9, 1988

■

Inhuman label risks
loss of caring adults

IT WAS THE WORD "BEASTMASTERS" THAT STUCK IN MY MIND. Beastmasters.

It's not in the dictionary or the encyclopedia. In fact, I had never heard the word, never processed the syllables through my mind, until I came across the word in a Detroit News article.

The article dealt with the epidemic of slain children in Detroit. The piece gave some explanations for the violence; it offered some solutions. I read it, just as I have read Free Press articles on the same subject.

I'm not writing this column to compare stories. That's irrelevant. Only a fool would focus on professional rivalries when the issue is slaughtered children.

But I do want to talk about words and the power they wield, the way they're able to change things, give them different form and meaning. Words can turn into a stone wall to separate us, a laser to bloodlessly remove a malignancy, a lightning bolt to strip humanity from the soul just as it strips the bark from a tree.

And to me, the key word in the News story was beastmaster.

It was used to describe a hard-core group of young criminals who threaten the community with their violence and drugs. The word also showed up in one of those little headlines used to break up stretches of copy on a page. The reporters didn't coin the word. I checked. Though I had not heard it before, it was readily recognized by some of the people who work in the juvenile justice system.

"It's part of the vernacular of the street culture," a juvenile worker explained to me. Youngsters use it to describe the enforcer in a gang, the disciplinarian, the one who does the killing.

Beastmaster. That's a frightening word to attach to a human being. It's not the kind of term one would use to describe a child or a loved one or even a passing acquaintance. No. It's a word that repels, a word that rebuffs attempts at closeness and communication, a word that curls up in

117

the air like a foul smell.

We need to beware of words like this, lest they invade our conversations and begin to alter the way we view our young people. We need to beware, lest they make it easier for us to separate ourselves completely from those troubled young criminals whom we don't understand and cannot control.

We need to beware because the more we distance ourselves from these young people, the easier it becomes to view them as a breed apart from us, a different species, an alien presence.

And once we have completely severed the ties between us, once we have willfully blinded ourselves to our children's humanity, then we can march inexorably toward the conclusion that these monsters/beastmasters/outlaws must be caged, even destroyed, to save the community.

Beastmaster.

Once we have built the walls and flung the lightning bolts, we will be able to accept the destruction of a segment of our young, a segment we really don't like very much if we're honest enough to admit it.

But, even though we dislike and fear these young criminals, do we really want to begin through our use of language to position ourselves to accept their destruction?

That's just what we do when we refer to them as less than human.

Look, I'm not arguing that we should coddle all of these young people who terrorize us and cause us so much pain. We need justice. We need swift and sure punishment.

But we also need to remember that a human being, not a beast, lives beneath the layers of labels we are tempted to drape over the swaggering shoulders of these young people.

I just happen to believe that we can punish the guilty without stripping them of their humanity; that we can wrestle with seemingly unsolvable problems without despising the youngsters who leave them at our door.

Heck, I even believe we're smart enough to damn words like "beastmaster" without damning the human beings who fashion them from the seething impotence of their lives.

February 27, 1989

■

Cocaine addicts are a lot like us

THE SIX OF THEM SAT IN A RAGGED CIRCLE IN A LITTLE ROOM JUST off the drug treatment ward.

They had come together to talk about their addiction to crack cocaine and their continuing battle to stay clean, or "alive," as one person said.

Recovering addicts, they were members of an outpatient support group run by Lifeline, a cocaine treatment program operated out of Northwest General Hospital in Detroit. Some had been clean for months, others for weeks.

I don't know what I expected, but I didn't expect what I found. I didn't expect to look around the room and see bits and pieces of myself and my family and friends in folks whom I had thought of as "them."

Crack addicts are young, right? You see them, nothing more than babies, really, riding around in Jeeps or pickup trucks or walking around with beepers attached to their belts. Crack addicts are derelicts, right? Dirty, unemployed thieves and whores.

Well, some addicts are painfully young and some are street hustlers, but these folks weren't. Most aren't, according to the experts.

Three of the people in that ragged circle were breathing hard on middle age, one was 31, one was flirting with 30, and one was 25. Three held down blue-collar jobs, three had white-collar ones. They had families and relationships, credit cards, checking accounts, college courses under their belts.

One man worked as a computer operator and earned $600 a week. The only woman in the group worked at a utility company; she and her husband had a household income of $60,000.

The 31-year-year auto dealership employee pulled down $40,000 a year. His wife worked, too.

Because they were smart, they all knew how to juggle the checks and credit cards and the loans from friends. They had done it to keep the money flowing after their paychecks had curled up in smoke.

They had other things in common, too. Each started using drugs — alcohol or marijuana — early. Most by the age of 13, one at age 6. Most grew up in families where drugs caused problems. And they all had lied to themselves about their addiction. They told themselves that they controlled this "classy" drug until the drug told them otherwise. And then they wanted to die, each one of them.

A 41-year-old General Motors Corp. employee drove his car into a tree when he was "high as a rainbow" and tired of living.

A 34-year-old factory worker who had been in two previous treatment programs went on a three-day, $3,000 binge. He tried to smoke himself to death so he wouldn't have to face his wife. He almost succeeded.

A 28-year-old woman "played out all the games, the credit cards, the checks, the friends." She considered suicide when her whole life went out of her control.

These folks weren't kids. They weren't dumb. They certainly weren't derelicts. "I worked hard to get the money to get high," a group member said. "I never stole," added another. "I misappropriated some funds."

Of course, if they had stayed with the drug, they might have done all the things you read about. Or they might have died.

"I took my kids' money. . . . I took my wife's money. . . . I missed work. . . . My full-time job was getting high. . . . I wanted to die."

But they didn't die. They are recovering addicts, or as the jargon goes, addictive personalities trying to stay clear of the lure of this highly addictive drug with its long, long memory.

"We are proof that there is life after death," said one group member. The others agreed, including those who repeatedly have been unable to resist the lure of a drug that beckons them in their dreams.

A Lifeline executive said that 60 percent to 70 percent of those who go through treatment manage to stay clean. The follow-up groups are a key to success.

"People can recover," said the woman in the group. "It's important that people know that."

It's also important to remember that a lot of folks in that room — and in rooms around the city — are more like us than "them."

March 3, 1989

■

Crime summit is a disappointment

DEAR MAYOR YOUNG:

I wish I didn't have to say this, but the crime summit was — with one important exception — a disappointment.

I didn't know exactly what to expect. But, because I have for years admired your wit, strength and matchless ability to rally the troops, I thought you again would dazzle us with your ideas and set the tone and direction for an attack on crime.

I wanted that to happen, I really did. I chided you about holding an invitation-only summit, and you responded by turning no one away. I hoped that was a good sign, because I wanted the summit to succeed.

I wanted it to work for selfish reasons. Hell, I live in the city, and, unless I divorce my husband — your biggest supporter, by the way — I will probably never leave Detroit, because he ain't going no place.

I wanted the summit to be a smashing success because I have a teenage son who will be home from school this summer. I want him and his friends to be safe on the streets.

I wanted it to succeed because I know that a lot of people wanted it to fail, for all kinds of reasons. For some, it's probably your politics. For others, it's your style and, for still others, it's because you're an outspoken old bird who isn't afraid to peck at the eyes of the very devil himself.

I expected the summit to succeed because I remember how you rallied the community in 1984 during the schoolgirl rape crisis. You laid out plans for action and, as one participant at both sessions said, you gave us marching orders and made us feel that concrete things would be done.

You announced the Eyes and Ears program, whereby utility workers joined the battle against rape. You deployed helicopters and police officers all over the place. You fired people up. Citizens got involved.

This summit lacked direction and energy.

The highlight was the announcement about plans by the city and the school system to establish facilities to rehabilitate youngsters who carry guns in school or who have been convicted of felonies.

When you talked about the plans for those youth facilities, the old spark was there. The audience perked up and applauded. Didn't you feel the electricity? When you vowed to get the money and to have something working by July 1, you had the audience in your hand.

But that was it. Sure, it was good to hear you call for more citizen involvement, and everyone is pleased that you will get even more police from behind their desks and onto the streets within a month.

But that just wasn't enough, Mr. Mayor. The first full hour of the summit was a recitation on police success stories, training procedures and improved communications systems that will cut down on emergency response time.

I'm glad our police are well trained. I, too, think we have a fine department. I'm glad we have a beefed-up 911 system.

But folks didn't go to Veterans Memorial to hear that. They went to get marching orders. They went to get charged up for the battle.

Look, I know you're ticked off at the Detroit News for a series of articles on the Police Department. I know it must be frustrating to read stories that you consider to be lies and to be unable to get the same newspaper space to rebut those stories. But, as irritating as that may be, folks didn't come down downtown to hear you criticize the Detroit News.

Folks came to be energized by that Coleman Young magic.

It wasn't there. I'm telling you this because I have a feeling that people around you may be afraid to do so.

I'm telling you this because you need to know.

I'm telling you this because I believe in you and I believe — if this fight is going to be won, if we are to do all we can do — you have to lead us with vigor and purpose and energy.

Most of all, I'm telling you this because you are my mayor, and this is my city, and I'll be damned if I'll sit back and accept less than a first-rate performance from a man who has been, and could be again, the best mayor in the country.

Violence finds way
into child's world

IN A WAY, SHE IS LIKE THE NEIGHBORHOOD DOLL, A QUIET, PRETTY 2-year-old with soft brown hair and delicate features.

It was not unusual for the older children on the street, particularly the big girls, to stop by her house on the way to the store or the playground and ask if they could take her along.

It also was not unusual for her big brother and his friend to take her up to the store with them to buy candy.

No one thought anything of it.

She lives on a block with more children than houses, a block where knots of teens gather across the street from a boarded-up house and where toddlers play in the shadow of yet another boarded-up house.

Children everywhere.

And that's probably why no one in that west side neighborhood found it unusual when, according to police, her brother's friend took her from the playground just a block and a half from her home and carried her off.

The friend, 15, had spent a lot of time at the girl's home. He had eaten at her family's table. He was, the little girl's aunt said, like a member of the family. The little girl knew his name and she trusted him because he was part of her world.

But that day, the little girl's world went crazy. According to court records, she was taken by that friend to an abandoned house half a mile from her home. Once there, according to official reports, she was raped and sodomized repeatedly by the 15-year-old friend and by an 11-year-old neighbor.

Court records say she started crying when the attack began.

When it was over, she was tossed like a discarded toy into a beige metal trash bin in an alley just a few steps from the abandoned house. The lid was pushed down and she was left there, crying for help.

Strangers rescued her, took her to a nearby store and called the police. Other strangers took her to a hospital where even more strangers examined her, treated her and cared for her for three days until she was released in her aunt's custody.

From the time she was dumped in that trash bin until she went home with her aunt, all she saw were strangers. She didn't see anyone she

122

trusted. Because of that, a child psychologist said, she easily could have thought that she had done something bad and was being punished for it.

After all, adults have problems coping with rape. What do you expect from a 2-year-old? She continued to be traumatized even after the rape.

Police have charged the 15-year-old family friend and the 11-year-old neighborhood youth in the attack. A 67-year-old man, accused by the family friend of forcing the youngsters to rape the child, has been released from custody because of insufficient evidence. But the investigation is continuing into his possible involvement.

As the aunt was taking the child home from the hospital, the little girl touched her aunt's fingernail and then touched a cut on her own finger. "---- (the family friend) hurt me," she said in a tiny voice. "----- hurt me."

Experts say that rape of little children is not rare in this city or this country. This attack was unusual only in its extremes — the dumping in the trash and the still questionable involvement of the 67-year-old man.

At least 20,000 children 5 and younger were sexually abused in this country in 1986, according to the most recent figures available from the American Humane Association, a Denver-based child advocacy group. That figure is conservative, based on 27 states that report sex abuse by age. Factor in the other states, and the figure easily could reach 30,000.

One of every four sexually assaulted juveniles is of kindergarten age or younger.

"Tell people, especially mothers, to pay attention when their children say someone hurt them," a local rape counselor said.

"Tell them," she said, "that it happens, over and over."

The 15-year-old pleaded guilty and was sentenced to a juvenile facility until his 21st birthday.

May 24, 1989

■

Gun-toting adults
shoot laughs down

HEAVEN HELP ME, I'VE LOST MY SENSE OF HUMOR.

To tell the truth, I am so forgetful that I didn't realize it was gone until I reached for it Tuesday morning and couldn't find it any place.

At first I assumed I simply had misplaced it. That happens a lot.

I lose my car keys at least once a week and my glasses biweekly. At least once a year, I put the salt box in the refrigerator and the half-empty preserves jar in the cabinet over the stove.

Absentmindedness runs in my family.

123

My grandmother once loaded the bathroom sink with dirty dishes and my mother forgot what she'd named me. Actually, she didn't forget, she just reversed the names, leading me to labor for 16 years under the belief that my middle name was my first. Informed of her mistake, she said 16 years wasn't that long; I had kept her in the delivery room twice that long.

So, realizing my genetic predisposition for losing things, I searched all the usual places: under the bed, my purse, my desk, the washing machine and the dirty clothes chute. I found a half-eaten candy bar, $1.73 in change and a 10-year-old test paper my son got a perfect score on.

The test paper was preserved in the clothes chute where it would have rested undisturbed for another 10 years without the search. The loose change was in the washing machine as partial payment for all the socks the machine has devoured over the years. The candy was stashed under the bed just in case we are invaded in the middle of the night by aliens who are afraid of chocolate.

Yes, I looked all over for my sense of humor. Then I had a terrible thought. What if it was lost forever? What if I threw it away with the junk mail and month-old spaghetti sauce?

I'd be devastated. Honest. Would I ever be able to find someone to laugh at the obvious flaws in the dressing room mirror as I tried on a two-piece bathing suit?

I didn't realize how serious the loss was until I started reading a newspaper story about a Chicago-based company that takes folks on a two-hour sight-seeing tour of sites connected with the Windy City's gangster past.

Called Untouchable Tours, the itinerary includes the theater where John Dillinger was killed by FBI agents. The tour costs $17.

According to the newspaper account, Untouchable Tours is "a small-time family operation combining acting, humor and well-researched history."

Where does the humor enter? In addition to the ride, the story said, the tourists are given plastic machine guns for mowing down would-be bad guys or just plain bad drivers.

" 'I need a bus driver shot over here,' the tour guide announced as they rode along Michigan Avenue in search of Chicago's gangster-era past.

"The tourists happily aimed and shot.

"Rat-a-tat-tat. A dozen plastic machine guns sputtered from windows of the Untouchable Tours bus.

"The targeted CTA driver, shot for road hogging, couldn't help but smile."

The article even had a big picture of tourists leaning out the bus windows with grins on their faces and toy machine guns in their hands.

Doggone it. Those folks looked like they were having so much fun playing killer that I took one last stab at trying to locate my sense of humor.

I rifled through my desk and stumbled across the latest copy of the Anti-Handgun Association newsletter. Maybe it got stuck in one of the pages.

Wrong. All I found was an open letter from the Rev. Thomas Lumpkin, an association board member, who takes part in the anti-handgun vigil each Monday at noon in front of the City County Building.

"In the next weeks," he wrote, "we will undertake the sad but, unfortunately, not difficult task of 'updating' the meditation booklet used at the vigil to report statistics and recount tragedies of the past year."

I guess a sense of humor is not the worst thing you can lose these days.

June 14, 1989

■

They're ours —
each one of them

SOMEHOW IT DOESN'T FEEL QUITE RIGHT TO COMPARE THEM because they were so different in mood and structure and expectation. But each event was held to celebrate the same thing: that annual rite of passage known as the high school graduation ceremony.

Both ceremonies were wonderful. Bright-eyed kids with butterflies in their stomachs. Parents so proud they couldn't stop smiling.

Still. . . .

One graduation was in the northern suburbs, the other in Detroit. One was for a private school, the other for a public one.

One was viewed as yet another step in a long-planned journey to college and probably graduate school. The other was seen as a mighty leap across a chasm that had claimed too many young people.

June 2, 1989. The 204 young women from the Mercy High School Class of 1989 walked across the stage at Oakland University's Baldwin Pavilion to accept their diplomas. The graduates wore white dresses, some billowing to the ground in clouds of organdy and lace, others stopping smartly at mid-calf. Sprigs of baby's breath occasionally peeked out from coils of hair and each young woman cradled a bouquet of long-stemmed red roses in her arms. It was lovely.

Mercy describes itself as a Catholic college preparatory school for young women. And that's exactly what it is.

Considered one of the finest schools in the area, Mercy attracts bright, determined young women, most of whom come from middle-class homes. Tuition runs about $3,500 a year, and about half the families have to struggle to pay the fees. One in 13 students is on partial scholarship.

The racially mixed school stresses social responsibility and academic excellence. About 95 percent of graduates go off to college.

June 12, 1989. The Charles E. Chadsey High School graduating class marched in cap and gown down the center aisle of the Scottish Rite Cathedral in the Masonic Temple in Detroit. The red and gold school colors stood out like victory flags in the sober, high-ceiling room.

"We are here. We did it. We survived," the bold colors seemed to say.

The graduating class had 229 seniors. Their names were neatly typed on the program. But if you could go back four years, back to the time when the Class of 1989 entered Chadsey as ninth graders, you would find twice as many students.

About half the class dropped out of school somewhere along the way, a school official explained. The biggest drop occurred immediately after the ninth grade. Youngsters who already were three, maybe four years behind decided that school was not for them. That's true for Chadsey and true for most big city public schools.

Located in southwest Detroit, Chadsey draws a mix of students from different racial and cultural backgrounds. What unites most of them is economics.

As factories around it have shut down, more and more of Chadsey's students have come from homes that rely on public assistance. And, in a good number of the Chadsey homes, the 1989 graduating senior was among the first of the family members — if not the first — to finish high school.

Before the diplomas were handed out at Mercy's graduation, parents and friends were asked to hold their applause. Some did; most didn't. The names of graduates were greeted with localized bursts of polite applause — occasionally a few cheers.

The same request was made at the Chadsey graduation. But no one paid it any mind. Parents rushed down front to get pictures. Some waited at the foot of the stairs to embrace their children. The cathedral was filled with round after round of cheers.

"That's my baby! That's my baby!" shouted a mother standing directly in front of the stage, camera in hand, smile on her face.

And she was right. Not just about her child, but about all of them.

From Mercy to Chadsey and from Detroit to Farmington Hills, they are all our babies, our children, our graduates, our future.

126

∎

How many deaths
does it take till . . .

A DETROIT PUBLIC SCHOOL TEACHER CALLED TO ASK IF I KNEW THE
agreed-upon number of dead youngsters that Detroiters are willing to
accept each year without rising up to stop the killings.

"What's the number?" he asked. "How many dead kids are OK? Fifty,
60, 70?"

The teacher didn't expect an answer. He just needed to hurl the
question. Death and ruined lives seemed to be following him like a shadow.
He couldn't get away from them.

As it turned out, the teacher knew both the 7-year-old girl who was
shot to death while playing on her front porch and the 15-year-old boy who
was the intended victim of the shooting.

In case you somehow missed the story, here's what happened.

The little girl, Tommie McClendon, was shot in the head, and two
other youngsters were wounded when a group of youths on bicycles
opened fire as the children played on the front porch in the 5700 block of
16th Street on the west side.

The young gunmen didn't set out to kill the little girl, but don't take any
false comfort from that fact. According to police reports, the bike riders
were trying to shoot a 15-year-old who lives near the house where the
children were playing.

The bikers reportedly belonged to a group or gang called the
Untouchables; the intended victim belonged to a rival one called the Zone
Eights. I have no idea what the feud was about. I wouldn't be at all
surprised if the reason was astoundingly insignificant.

The shooting pushed the teacher over the edge of comprehension.

He knew the little girl as a nice, happy child. He couldn't tell me much
about her, other than to say that she was seven years old. He mentioned
her age as if it explained everything. "She was a baby," he said.

A few years back, the teacher knew the intended victim as a quiet
elementary school student who was a slow learner. The young man
needed lots of extra help and attention, more than the schools were
equipped to give him. The youngster's family tried to keep him out of
trouble and wound up in a tug of war with the streets, the teacher said.
The youngster was the prize. If police reports are correct, the streets won
when the youngster found identity and recognition in the Zone Eights.

The teacher said he didn't know the youngsters in custody in the fatal
shooting. I don't know them, either, but I'm willing to bet their lives differ

only in degree from that of the intended victim.

Maybe, the teacher said, if we adults had spent more time and energy with the intended victim and the alleged shooters when they were younger, the little girl might not be dead. The youngsters arrested in the shooting might not be in trouble.

The teacher also said that, unless we get serious about saving these kids while they are young, we will be doomed. We never will be able to build enough jail cells or juvenile camps to imprison them when they are older.

The tragedy that haunts that teacher should haunt all of us.

According to Free Press statistics, the little girl was among 20 youngsters under 17 shot to death in Detroit as of that day. Two hours after the little girl was shot, a 14-year-old youth was killed in a separate incident. The 14-year-old was shot outside an east side house when, according to police, a youth in his late teens ran by and opened fire.

The number of children shot, but not fatally wounded, stood at 105 by the end of that day.

But back to the original question: What's the accepted number?

Darned if I know.

But, as I searched for an answer, I came across these numbers.

In Michigan, about $620 million a year is spent to lock up or to monitor convicted criminals. About one tenth of that is spent on various preschool and Head Start programs for our children.

Neither place has enough room to hold all those who need to be there.

June 28, 1989

■

Little electric chair for small-fry killers

MY FRIEND VI CALLED. SHE WANTED TO KNOW IF EXECUTIONERS would special-order electric chairs for 7-year-olds or just modify those funny combination desk-chairs that kids sit at in second grade.

Vi was trying to decide if she should keep the old wooden one she bought years ago or get rid of it at her annual yard sale.

"If I sold it I'd probably get 10 times what I paid for it," she said.

"So sell it," I told her. "Take the money and we'll go to lunch."

"But, if I sell it, what if it winds up on death row in some prison? What if some little kid sits down thinking it's time for milk and cookies, and instead gets zapped with a zillion volts of electricity? I couldn't live with myself."

As usual, I had no idea what Vi was talking about. I figured she'd been into the vanilla extract again.

So I told her that nobody executes 7-year-old children. A few get caught by stray bullets now and then, but the government doesn't fry little fish.

Vi wasn't buying any of that argument. She had just learned that the U.S. Supreme Court ruled that states can execute mentally retarded murderers and juveniles who were as young as 16 when they committed their crimes.

Teenagers who aren't old enough to enlist in the Army are old enough to get the death penalty. A murderer with the mental function of a little child can be executed as long as the jury and judge take into account the killer's intellectual deficiencies when reaching a life or death verdict.

The mental retardation ruling was based on a Texas case involving a convicted rapist and murderer who had an IQ of about 60 and the mental capacity of a 7-year-old. A jury in Texas sentenced the man to death.

The Supreme Court set aside that sentence because the jury hadn't given enough consideration to the man's mental retardation. But the guy could be sentenced to death again if a new proceeding met the Supreme Court's test.

Vi was distraught.

"If the court says it's OK to kill an adult who functions on the level of a 7- or 8-year-old, who's to say those judges won't decide next year that it's OK to kill a pain-in-the butt 8- or 10-year-old — or maybe a 13-year-old — with an IQ of 140 and the mental capacity of a 16-year-old?"

I told Vi that no sane, logical and compassionate nation would kill kids that young.

"And where's the logic here?" she demanded. "Why is it not OK to kill a 7-year-old mind in a 7-year-old body while it is OK to kill a 7-year-old mind in a 25- or 30-year-old body?

"Does the court ruling mean there's a height and weight requirement for the death penalty these days? And who the hell can draw a meaningful intellectual or physical difference between 15- and 16-year-old kids?"

There was no stopping her. I tried to explain that the majority opinion in both rulings declared that our society doesn't have what lawyers call a national consensus against executing 16-year-olds and the mentally retarded. Since there is no consensus against it, it isn't cruel and unusual punishment.

Then I reminded Vi that the court in a 4-3 decision last year overturned the death penalty for a 15-year-old. Plus, even the death penalty opponents don't think these rulings will result in a rash of executions of the young or the mentally impaired.

"Yeah, sure," she sneered. "Let me tell you something, Ms. National Consensus.

"Average folks have had it up to here with vicious young criminals. As younger and younger kids get involved in violent crimes, the high and mighty national consensus about the age for execution is going to drop like a stone.

"Today it's 16. Next year it could be 15. God forbid what it will be 10 years from now," she said.

"Vi," I said, "you're exaggerating. You're dealing in hyperbole again."

"Well, I'll tell you what I'm not dealing in," she said.

"What?"

"School desks."

4

EQUALITY

'Too many of us' running away?

A FRIEND CALLED AND, IN THE COURSE OF THE CONVERSATION, mentioned that she had moved into Dearborn.

"Interesting," I said. "So you're one of the handful of black folks out there now? How do you like it?"

"It's quiet and peaceful," she said. "I love it."

She went on to explain that her apartment building has strict income requirements and that all the tenants are gainfully employed or independently comfortable.

But there was one problem.

"Since I've been here," she said, "it seems like nothing but blacks are moving in. When I moved in, there were hardly any of us here. Now there are too many of us."

I guess if any more blacks move into the complex, my friend would have to start apartment hunting again. She'd be looking for a place where once again she is safely in the minority.

The next morning, I mentioned the conversation to a co-worker, who happens to be Jewish. Before I could get to the punch line, my co-worker shook her head and huffed a laugh that had nothing funny in it.

She had heard the same kind of remarks about "too many Jews" from her Jewish friends. It has nothing to do with education or economic status, she said. It's just that the presence of too many Jews makes some other Jews uncomfortable.

I'll bet the same thing holds true for other groups that have over time been singled out and abused because of their race or religion.

"Too many of us." What an intriguing concept. Too many for what? For dinner? For a game of bridge? For a barbecue on the patio? For a PTA meeting? For invisibility? For comfort? For forgetting?

I'll leave that answer to the sociologists and psychologists and all those other ologists out there. They can explain in great and boring detail exactly why my friend feels threatened by the presence of a number of folks who look like her and earn approximately the same money.

As for me, I'm wondering about the flip side of my friend's comment.

I wonder, for example, how often WASPS, white Anglo-Saxon Protestants, talk about moving out of their neighborhoods because there are too many other WASPS around.

It happens, I'm sure. But gut instinct and a sense of history make me believe that it's not a really common occurrence.

133

Dollars to doughnuts, Joe or Jane WASP isn't greeted at home in the evening by a husband or wife who demands that they start looking for a new place to live because there are just "too many of us."

And it's not just WASPs — not by a long shot. Take any group that perceives itself as being in a favored or preferred situation, and you probably won't find a lot of folks in that group complaining about the presence of "too many of us."

C'mon. Think about it.

How many so-called "non-impaired" folks do you think start house hunting solely because they live in a neighborhood where there are no group homes for the mentally ill or the developmentally disabled?

It's hard to imagine a conversation where someone says: "We've got to put the house up on the market because there are too many of us non-mentally ill, non-developmentally disabled people around."

And it's just as hard to conceive of people running away from an area solely because there are too many families who own their own homes or too many families who have a little money in the bank. Who runs away solely because there are too many people with decent cars, too many families with a steady income? Who leaves solely because the schools are too good or the city services too reliable?

Do the people who sees themselves as society's favored children flee from their own kind because there are "too many of us"?

Or, perhaps, is that the reaction of people who have broken the shackles on their feet but still carries them in their minds?

Like I said, I'll leave the answers to the experts. I'm just wondering when I'll have to learn a new phone number for my friend.

June 18, 1986

■

What does it feel like to be white?

I WONDER WHAT IT FEELS LIKE TO BE WHITE. I HAVE NO IDEA, BUT I am, on occasion, curious.

I've never, on the other hand, found myself wondering what it feels like to be male, although I have wanted in times of stress to have bulging biceps so I could knock an adversary flat on his back.

But white is something else again. I wonder if the collective white experience, if indeed there is such a thing, can be probed, explored and subjected to the same kinds of generalizations that routinely are applied to the collective black experience?

I doubt it. Still, I can't resist the temptation to ask, in a general way, some questions that come from my experience.

I wonder if little white girls played with little black dolls whose hair had to be oiled and straightened into submission? Of course, that's an unfair question. Little black girls didn't play with those dolls either. We played with pink or brown cloth-bodied babies whose hair could be brushed and teased into big fat curls.

Kinky hair, mahogany skin, thick lips and a wide nose were not things you paid money for. No. You paid money to straighten your hair, to lighten your skin, to buy a lip liner to make your lips look smaller. I started thinking about all of this after I was given a new face by an extremely nice makeup artist who brushed dark powder down the sides of my nose to narrow it and then outlined my lips in brown to give them less substance and more form.

Somehow, I never thought my lips would become a metaphor for life.

In any event, I wonder what it would feel like to walk into the Free Press one day and be a member of the majority population?

I wonder what it would feel like to walk into a General Motors management meeting or to go into a restaurant in Traverse City and see your skin tone repeated over and over again throughout the room?

I wonder what it feels like to walk into an office or store filled with white shoppers and not feel out of step, if only for a second?

I wonder what it feels like never to have been told: "I never think of you as black."

I wonder what it feels like to go through an entire week at work without being asked:

■ My opinion on a black political or social situation.

■ The name of a black expert on a particular subject.

■ If a story is racially significant.

I wonder what it feels like to go on vacation, get a deep tan, walk up to a black person and put your tanned arm next to that black arm and say: "See how dark I am? We're almost the same color."

I wonder what it feels like to have someone ask what nationality your parents are?

I wonder what it feels like to be able to go to almost any movie at any time and see people who look like you up on the screen — to see loving, laughing, fighting, heroic or cowardly people, each one reflecting an aspect of humanity. I've often thought that the controversy over "The Color Purple" really stemmed from the fact that blacks are woefully underrepresented in movies. Thus, every "black" movie becomes a statement about black life and is given greater significance than it deserves.

I wonder what it feels like to set up a lunch date with a stranger at a fancy restaurant in some upscale suburb and have to give a detailed description about what you'll be wearing and the color of your hair?

Perhaps there are no answers to these questions. Perhaps the inherent generalizations make them meaningless.

Still, I do wonder — about the questions and about the responses I'll get from those folks, black and white, who think they know the answers.

October 1, 1984

■

She gave support to two households

SHE'S THE ONE WHO TOLD ME TO CHERISH THOSE DAYS WHEN MY child was too young to feed himself, when he demanded attention during his every waking hour.

She's the one who could coax a smile out of a sulky child and who turned the simple act of hugging a toddler into a feast of giggles and clucks and deep murmurings between the two of them.

I thought about her this morning as I read an article about career women who juggled motherhood and professions long before mothers became so common in the workplace.

Two of the women — a lawyer and a doctor — credited supportive husbands and reliable housekeepers for their successes. The housekeepers became surrogate mothers. They cooked, washed, darned, ironed, counseled, kissed away hurts and nursed children too sick for school.

One woman in the article, now a New York State Supreme Court justice, had six kids between 1942 and 1953 and still worked full time. "Without an affluent husband, it couldn't be done," she said in the article. "We couldn't find day care, and if we had we would have been condemned."

Her comments left me breathless. For most of my life I've known and lived around women who have worked as housekeepers or domestics. And, almost invariably, their employers eventually referred to them as invaluable, adored, part of the family. Even their names changed. Mary became Our Mary, Hazel became Our Hazel, Nell . . . Our Nell.

The affection, I am sure, was genuine and was most often returned in equal measure.

But I am struck by something that seems to have escaped general scrutiny in that article.

This wonderful person who allowed someone else to fullfill herself — this treasure who slipped into another woman's kitchen at 6:30 a.m. — was the same person who slipped out of another house earlier, probably a

136

house with children who also needed tending and counseling and a little extra loving, floors that needed mopping, food that needed cooking and laundry that neither cleaned nor ironed itself.

"Our Nell" left her children to take care of another woman's children.

And while the professional woman-mother-wife in the article juggled the often conflicting demands of home and the workplace, I wonder if the housekeepers were doing the same juggling act, only without a husband to lean on and a housekeeper to rely on?

I was reminded of all the women I have known who have worked for generations, not decades, caring for other people's children while they prayed that their own kids would be safe.

My friend, who coaxes smiles from sulky children, raised at least two families — her own and her employer's. She retired in her late 60s.

She worked because she had to work. She couldn't lean on her husband, the children's father, for support, and so she did the only work she knew how to do. She taught her kids to take care of themselves and prayed they learned their lessons well.

Perhaps that's why she always reminded me to enjoy the time I had with my child. She knew what the loss of that time meant.

She was part of one family where children were so special they could not be left alone, and she was head of another family where equally special children had to be left alone if the family was to survive. She nurtured the first; she lived for the second.

"It was a way of life," she said. "You don't stop and analyze it. If you had taken time to analyze it, you would have fallen apart. You had no choice."

Today her own children are grown, with children and grandchildren of their own. The other people's children are also grown.

Through it all, the irony of her existence never escaped her, even if she didn't have time to analyze it.

She was part of their family all right — but they were never part of hers.

June 14, 1985

■

What price glory?
$21,500 plus dues

INTERCEPTED LETTERS ...
Dear Ann Flanders: What's a body to do?
My husband and I joined the Oakland Hills Country Club last year with

the expectation that we would, by virtue of our membership, become top flakes on the upper crust.

You know about Oakland Hills in Bloomfield. It's the site this week of the U.S. Open and it's positively the place to be.

Well, we gladly paid our $21,500 initiation fee and we shell out $205 in monthly dues to support the magnificent grounds and the white frame clubhouse with its bright green shutters and deep red roses.

The club has scads of doctors and lawyers as members, a good number of corporate executives and even an aging jock or two. Oakland Hills has your basic God-fearing, decent Christian white person who doesn't ask for handouts and who carries his own load, most of the time. We do have, of course, a few people of the Jewish persuasion as members, but most members probably couldn't tell them from anyone else.

We don't have any black members, of course. I happen to think blacks would rather stay with their own kind. Anyway, we paid all that membership money so we could go someplace and forget the problems of the world. Of course, Oakland Hills isn't alone in lacking black members. Lots of clubs don't have them. After all, that's why we call them social clubs instead of civil rights groups.

We do, however, have black employees at the club, and they are swell people. In fact, all of our staff members, black and white, are super. Our president really hit the nail on the head when he mentioned our employees in a recent newspaper article about the club. He said: "I view them almost like members. You know they're special when the waitress who picked up the crumbs from the floor under your little girl's high chair is the same one who served champagne at that little girl's wedding 20 years later."

I couldn't agree more. I feel about staff the same way I feel about the cleaning girl who took care of me as a baby and who now cleans for my married daughter. She's part of the family.

Oh, but back to my problem. Well, everybody at the club was positively ecstatic over the fact that we landed the U.S. Open golf tournament this week. Talk about upscale. I'll bet those other clubs were eating their hearts out. Then the roof fell in.

The same newspaper article that mentioned our staff also said that Golf Digest recently rated our club near the the middle of the social ladder of private clubs in the Detroit area.

Well, of course, both club president Charlie Hrdlicka and Maggie Allesee, editor of the club's magazine, took issue with the rating. "People think of the top two non-Jewish clubs, at least for snob appeal, as Bloomfield Hills (Country Club) and the Country Club of Detroit (in Grosse Pointe Farms). I really think Oakland Hills is next," Allesee said.

Well, Ann, we are shocked.

Next? What does she mean "next"? We have one of the highest membership fees around for our kind of people. Why aren't we on top instead of somewhere near the middle? Really, aren't our fees prohibitive enough to include us among the hoitiest of the toity? I already hold my nose so high up in the air that I run the risk of drowning when I go out in a rainstorm. Tell me, dear Ann, what price must my husband and I pay for admittance to the upper reaches of exclusivity, class and style? — A lesser snob.

Dear Lesser: Someone should have told you before you spent all that dough on membership fees that people who place a price tag on class and style will never have either one.

June 6, 1986

■

Prison statistics
recall old spiritual

THERE'S AN OLD SONG WE USED TO SING BACK IN THE '60S WHEN freedom and equality seemed just a demonstration away.

· We'd sit in a crowded church on a hot evening, trying to move the heavy air with cardboard fans donated by a local funeral parlor and we'd listen to the likes of Stokely Carmichael or Rap Brown talk about the struggle.

Rosa Parks, if she were there, would be asked to stand, and then the gathering would rise to applaud the tiny, soft-spoken woman whose courage ignited the civil rights movement. She'd reward us with a shy, self-conscious smile and then sit back down.

During the evening, as people would sing and nod and shout "amen," the feeling of freedom was in the air. It was palpable — as heavy and expectant as the cologne fanned from the bosom of a heavily-powdered sister who tried to cool herself in the heat of freedom's fire.

One of the most popular songs at those meetings was an old spiritual first sung years and years ago by black men and women whose yearning for freedom could never be chained or beaten into submission.

The song is called, "Oh, Freedom." I found myself thinking of the words to that spiritual a few days ago when I finally got around to asking for some statistics I had been meaning to request for months.

I had procrastinated because I had a feeling the numbers would reveal a portion of our reality that we, like that sister in church, try to fan away.

That sister didn't succeed; neither will we.

The statistics that follow come from the Michigan Department of Education and from the main computer of the Michigan Department of Corrections. Some will argue that I am comparing apples and oranges;

others will say the numbers must not be allowed to stand alone without benefit of explanation.

Well, apples and oranges are close enough kin for me, and I'm just too dispirited by the numbers right now to call experts and have them give long and surely valid socioeconomic reasons for them.

And so I'll simply give you the stats and you can make of them what you will. You can even try to fan them away, if you like.

There are more black men in Michigan's prison system than there are in Michigan's four-year colleges.

There were 6,066 black men in those colleges in the 1984-85 school year and 9,016 black men in prisons, prison camps and halfway houses as of October 1985.

Now, you'll probably argue apples and oranges. Different years and age groups. Well, I've always thought it silly for passengers on a ship to quibble over a deck position when the thing is sinking.

But for those who demand more parallel figures, the prison population outnumbers the college population, even when you look at what could be considered "college age" men.

There are 6,105 black men ages 18 to 32 in our prison system. The prisoners edge out the college kids by 39 bodies.

Black men account for 5.3 percent of the male enrollment in four-year schools and for 56.2 percent of the prison population. For all 18-to-34-year-old men in the state, U.S. Census figures show that blacks account for 12.4 percent of the total population.

Black men also are over-represented in the ranks of the unemployed, the undereducated and the poor. That's been true for ages, even back in the 19th Century when the unquenchable thirst for freedom gave birth to the song that's been running through my head:

"Oh freedom, oh freedom, oh freedom over me, over me.

"And before I'd be a slave, I'll be buried in my grave

"And go home to my Lord and be free."

April 2, 1986

■

A white Goode
would be gone

JOE MADISON, NAACP EXECUTIVE AND LOCAL TALK SHOW HOST, SAID it on his radio show, and he was right.

If Philadelphia Mayor Wilson Goode had been white, the citizens of that city and indeed much of the nation would have demanded his resignation.

Last May, Philadelphia police tried to evict a radical group from a neighborhood by dropping a bomb on the group's headquarters. The bomb touched off a fire that resulted in the deaths of 11 people, including five children, and the destruction of 61 homes.

And police and fire department honchos allowed the fire to burn out of control for several hours as flames leaped from row house to row house.

It simply boggles the mind that this man could retain a political presence in that or any city after presiding over one of the fastest and bloodiest urban renewal projects in memory.

Immediately after the fire, Goode took full responsibility for the tragedy. Although he was not at the scene of the bombing, Goode said that the buck stopped at his desk.

His police chief and his managing director had his support and his backing, he said. And despite the deaths of 11 people who belonged to a radical group called MOVE, the community rallied behind the mayor.

Even after Goode started backtracking and heaping blame on his underlings for that colossal screwup, Philadelphians still supported him.

After all, it was said, Goode was a decent, God-fearing man who also happened to be the first black mayor in the City of Brotherly Love. Goode was no Frank Rizzo, whose eight-year mayoral reign in the 1970s was marked by charges of cronyism, corruption and racism. Goode was an educated, articulate man who represented Philadelphia's future.

And, after all, the MOVE group was a pain in the administration and the city. Involved in one fatal shootout with police in 1978, the group had terrorized a stable working-class neighborhood for about three years, fouling the streets and air with garbage and threats.

Oh, sure, some MOVE supporters railed against Goode and some community activists condemned him for failing to handle the crisis properly.

But even after Goode was accused of gross negligence by the investigatory commission he appointed in the wake of the MOVE affair, Philadelphians still did not rise up and demand that he resign.

I was unable to find one major business, civic or civil rights group in Philadelphia that had the guts to say that the first black mayor of Philadelphia should have gotten the hell out of office.

One of the city's journalists said part of the reluctance to call for Goode's resignation was the fact that the council president who, by law, would have replaced Goode was so sorry that he made Goode look like a political genius.

Another scribe said Philadelphians were tolerant because Goode's intentions were honorable, even if his actions were lamentable. He had a good heart and an empty head.

Well, folks, choose any excuse you want. You can't escape the fact that if Goode had been white, he would have been a political memory.

The city and probably the nation would not have allowed a white mayor to bomb that neighborhood and remain in office.

Yet, when a black man did just that, the City of Brotherly Love tap-danced all over the place, making excuses and apologizing, as if his color somehow tempered his gross negligence.

That was wrong; it simply was wrong. Just as the buck stopped on Goode's desk, the boot of civic and moral responsibility should have landed squarely on his seat of his power.

January 23, 1987

■

Let's put names and faces together

IT WOULD ALMOST BE FUNNY IF IT WEREN'T SUCH A DAMNED outrage.

A local Drug Enforcement Administration agent swore in an affidavit last week that he caught a glimpse — on television — of Michigan Supreme Court Justice Dennis Archer at a fund-raiser last year for Sen. Basil Brown.

Brown, as you know, has been going through legal hoops since he was arrested more than a year ago and charged by the Ingham County Prosecutor's Office with delivery and possession of small amounts of cocaine and marijuana.

The key witness against Brown is a drug-addicted prostitute who played footsie with the police to get the goods on the senator from Highland Park.

Brown has been arguing that he was entrapped by the police. His arguments were so forceful that the Supreme Court on Jan. 14 ordered a lower court to consider Brown's entrapment claim.

The very next day, the Ingham County Prosecutor's Office played its trump card. It filed the affidavit by DEA agent Scott Roberts in a bid to disqualify Archer from participating in Supreme Court consideration of the Brown matter.

The Prosecutor's Office stated that Archer should step down because "it appears that Justice Archer publicly has supported the defense of (Brown) on the charges which are at issue before this court."

In other words, folks, the prosecutor was saying that Justice Archer couldn't be fair because he was seen by a "witness" palling around with Brown at that Jan. 27, 1986, fund-raiser in Detroit.

Well, there's a small fly in the ointment.

142

Roberts' affidavit, which he filed as a private citizen, stated that he saw Archer on a Detroit newscast. He said he recognized him from earlier pictures he had seen. He also said the TV announcer had identified the justice on the air. Roberts refused to discuss the matter with me.

I called all four television stations — Channels 2, 4, 7 and 50 — that were there and not one could find any film of Archer at the Brown party. Hell, they had all looked. After all, it would have been a heck of a story.

Then, a news executive from WJBK (Channel 2) mentioned in passing that the film did contain a man who looked a lot like Archer, but wasn't him. Darned if the news executive from WKBD (Channel 50) didn't say the same thing. There's a guy on the tape who looks like Archer — black, balding, thin-faced — but isn't Archer, he said, and he never was identified as Archer.

So who was this mystery man that the DEA agent fingered? Well, the folks from Channels 2 and 50 say the Archer look-alike was Charles Beckham, the former Detroit water and sewerage director who was convicted in 1984 of racketeering, bribery and fraud.

Beckham's picture has been in the papers a lot, and — surprise, surprise — he says he was at the Brown fund-raiser. "I was there and the TV camera got a picture of me," he said. Beckham said he even saw himself on TV after the party.

Archer maintained he was not at the fund-raiser, and the Supreme Court rejected the DEA agent's claim. So where was Archer? He was attending a graduation ceremony at the Detroit College of Law and he was sitting on stage in front of a roomful of lawyers and law school grads.

All of which proves, I guess, that a certain DEA agent either needs to get glasses or needs to realize that looks and false assumptions can be deceiving.

Basil Brown pleaded guilty. He remained free pending his appeal.

March 23, 1988

■

A self-determined sign of the times

THIS IS A DAY LATE AND A DOLLAR SHORT, BUT WHAT THE HECK.

Read carefully the instructions for the following exercises and see if you can make the symbols described below.

Don't get all upset if you don't understand what you're doing — you know I wouldn't lead you astray.

Each step is a complete movement. Just keep practicing until you get each step right.

After you have mastered the first exercise, go to the second one. It's a little trickier, but you can do it.

Ready to start? Let's go.

Exercise 1

■ Clench your right hand into a fist and then raise that fist high into the air, like a victory sign.

■ Hold your right hand about 18 inches from your face with the palm turned toward you. Press baby and second fingers into your palm. Reach your thumb across your palm and place thumb on top of second finger. Rest your third finger on the tip of your thumb, remembering to keep straight. Point your fourth finger straight up in the air so that your third and fourth fingers form a "V."

■ Do the same thing with the left hand.

■ Place both hands close to the sides of your face and move hands in small circles, going back and forth.

There, that's the end of Exercise 1. Repeat until you can do the movements smoothly. Don't give up. Millions of men, women and children can do this.

Now, for the next exercise.

Exercise 2

■ Take the index finger of your right hand and press finger lightly against your left shoulder. In a smooth motion, bring right index finger across your chest and lightly touch your right shoulder.

■ Hold up your right hand with the palm parallel to your profile. Make sure your fingers are together. Brush the palm against your jaw, moving from the earlobe straight past your mouth as if you were wiping something off your face.

■ Clench both hands into tight fists and hold about chest high. Purposefully swing your right fist over the left one so that you end up with your right wrist resting on top of the wrist bone on your left hand.

That's it for Exercise 2.

What you have just done is what the former president of this nation's only liberal arts college for the deaf could not do when she was named to the job earlier this month. She could not sign, thus, she could not communicate with the students and some of the faculty at Gallaudet University in Washington, D.C.

After a week-long student protest that paralyzed the campus, the newly named president resigned. Three days later, the chairman of the board of trustees bowed to protests and resigned. And on that same day, the trustees appointed the first deaf president in Gallaudet's 124-year history.

Students now are demanding that at least half the 20-member

144

Gallaudet board be hearing impaired. Before the protest, only four board members had impaired hearing.

The Gallaudet protest was a struggle for the same kinds of things that all people want — dignity and equality. And the victory at this 2,100-student school represents much more than just a victory for a handful of college students, or even for the deaf and hearing impaired in this country. Gallaudet's victory means that yet another barrier to self-determination has come tumbling down.

Oh, by the way, if you're wondering what you said in sign language, here's the answer:

"Power to the People" and "We Shall Overcome."

Now, one last exercise. You really should stand up for this one.

Exercise 3

■ Take both hands, palms facing each other and hold them about a foot away from your face.

■ Forcefully bring hands together, pull apart and bring them back together in rapid, sharp movements. Go as quickly as you can for as long as you like.

■ Smile.

Wasn't that easy? You just gave the Gallaudet students a standing ovation.

April 5, 1989

■

Different standards shield U-M rioters

IT WAS "HAIL TO THE VICTORS" AND TO HELL WITH everything else Monday night on the University of Michigan campus.

Thousands of U-M fans celebrated the school's national basketball championship by engaging in a booze-fueled riot. The fans threw rocks and bottles into crowds, smashed plate-glass windows, slashed automobile tires, jumped up and down on cars, and then turned some over for good measure.

Eight people were arrested; dozens reportedly suffered minor injuries. One student said he was hit in the face when he tried to get some students off his car. Someone bopped a restaurant owner on the head and took $200 from his wallet as he tried to protect his business. A dozen fans tried to overturn a TV van.

And what, pray tell, do you think this violent, out-of-control mob of college-educated humanity was labeled by Ann Arbor police? Try "overzealous."

That's right, overzealous, as in "they really don't mean any harm" or "boys will be boys."

Well, thank heavens U-M is located in Ann Arbor.

If it were in an urban area like Detroit or Chicago or Miami, and if thousands of urban students conducted themselves like their 7,000 Wolverine counterparts, the event would have been called exactly what it was — a riot.

Had students from inner-city high schools behaved that way after a championship game, they would have been called rioters. Newspaper headlines would have screamed it; TV anchors would have proclaimed it.

And no amount of official sugarcoating would have changed it.

But the riot didn't happen in some troubled urban area. It happened in Ann Arbor, on a college campus. The kids involved were the offspring of the middle class or those who want to be middle class.

Different standards exist for these youngsters. When they riot, it's an aberration; when poor kids riot, it's an affirmation of what society has come to expect of them.

Well, buffalo chips.

Exuberance turned into violence in Ann Arbor. Fans — mainly students, police say — didn't just break the peace. They shattered it. Even if all those students in the streets weren't breaking windows and sailing bottles into crowds, they still were part of a riot.

And shame on 'em.

They know better. They aren't "underprivileged" youngsters who knock at the door of opportunity until their knuckles bleed and their spirit is covered with calluses. They are, so we are told, the cream of the crop. Well, all I can say is that this must have been one sorry year for crops.

But that's not all, not by a long shot.

I'd be willing to bet that most of those kids out there Monday night thought they were keeping alive the indomitable spirit that took that scrappy Michigan team to the top. Those students probably thought their high fives and victory whoops, their airborne bottles and rocks, transformed them, if only briefly, into Victors Valiant.

That just shows you what a lousy job we're doing of educating our kids.

The members of the Michigan basketball team didn't become victors just because their adrenalin was flowing. They became victors because of hard work, sweat, discipline and self-control.

They may have been charged up with emotion, but they played with precision born of years of dedication to a demanding and grueling sport.

And, after Michigan's heart-stopping win over Seton Hall, you didn't see the Michigan players throwing benches into the crowd or upending the scorekeeper's table or trying to shatter the backboard after they cut down the basketball net. No way.

They didn't do that because they knew it would cheapen their victory.

They also knew that U-M athletic director Bo Schembechler would have leapt from the stands and scared every last bead of sweat off their butts for acting like vandals, not victors.

On April 3, 1989, U-M won the NCAA championship against Seton Hall.

April 10, 1989

■

No excuse for slur, so kick my can

MY BOSSES FOOLISHLY BELIEVED YEARS AGO THAT I COULD LEARN to stop kicking over wastebaskets and yelling at the top of my voice when I was upset. So they sent me to a weeklong seminar in Miami, Fla., where I was supposed to learn how to handle problems better.

The participants were newspaper folks who, it was thought, would benefit from a course in communication and management skills.

To tell you the truth, we benefited more from the time we spent visiting Miami's nicest restaurants in the evening and watching the moon float over the water — all on expense accounts.

One of the seminar sessions dealt with the proper way for a boss to evaluate an employee. We were told to be straightforward and to document any criticism we offered.

The seminar leader, a really decent fellow, told us not to let the employee turn the tables and begin criticizing our failings.

Verbal retaliation should not be tolerated, he said.

Then, using a term he obviously had used before, he said: "Don't let them NIGGEYSOB you."

NIGGEYSOB was an acronym that, as best I recall, stood for "Now I'm Gonna Get Even, You SOB."

Well, I sat upright in my seat and said in a voice as hot as the flash of outrage that jolted my body: "I beg your pardon."

Where I come from, "I beg your pardon," said with the accent on the word "beg," means, "What the devil are you talking about and who do you think you are?"

Because there weren't any wastebaskets around, I proceeded to kick NIGGEYSOB from one end of the room to the other. I told the group leader that NIGGEYSOB was offensive to me as a human being, and anyone who was teaching other folks about management skills should know better than to use a term that sounded like the word "nigger."

My seminar leader was stunned. He said no one ever had a problem with the word before. The fact that it is offensive never even crossed his mind. He apologized, and I think the word was banished from future seminars.

I can't say that with authority because I never got a chance to attend another seminar down there. You see, I returned to Detroit and picked up where I had left off, kicking and yelling just like before.

Well, it's my turn to get kicked around for insensitivity. The Rev. Paul Nancarrow of Dearborn recently wrote the editor a letter about my use of a certain term in a column. I hope the letter will be printed on the editorial page because Mr. Nancarrow makes an important point.

Just to be sure you see it, let me reprint the letter here.

"I was surprised and dismayed that Susan Watson, a writer usually scrupulously sensitive to the ethnic and racial implications of her words, should so casually use an ethnic slur as she did in her column of March 29 (about some high school students who were bilked by a local travel agency). I refer to her use of the phrase 'welsh on the deal' not once, but twice.

"Surely Ms. Watson realizes that the people of Wales are no more inherently untrustworthy than other ethnic groups. Certainly she is too aware of anti-Semitism to say that a person who drove a hard bargain 'managed to Jew the price down'; nor can I imagine her denigrating Native Americans by calling someone who had second thoughts about a gift an 'Indian giver.' Why then her callous use of the name of an entire Celtic people to describe a deliberate default on a promise?

"If ethnic dignity is to be a reality for all, it must be applied to all."

Well, the only excuse I have is ignorance. And that wasn't good enough for me back in Miami; it shouldn't be good enough for Mr. Nancarrow now.

So, I apologize. And if the good reverend is a kicking man, he's got a standing invitation to visit my wastebasket.

August 23, 1989

■

Group home flap is hard to understand

LAW AND ORDER PREVAILED LAST WEEK IN TROY. BUT WHERE THE hell was decency?

A 25-year-old mentally handicapped man with an IQ of 21 and the intellectual capacity of a 3-year-old child could face a 90-day jail term and a $500 fine because he behaved like a 3-year-old.

It started when Mark Kubicki walked out of the group home where he lives and marched into a neighbor's home. Kubicki, who stands 6-foot-1 and weighs about 200 pounds, went into the kitchen, drank a glass of root beer, poured part of the bottle of pop down the drain and then drank about half a pot of cold coffee.

He didn't say anything. He couldn't. He's autistic. His conversation is limited to a few loud grunts and the word "no" when he doesn't want to do something.

The neighbor, Diane Greene, was in her kitchen when this stranger walked in. She was frightened. When the man started drinking the coffee, she thought he had to be insane.

Mark Kubicki is not insane. He's just mentally handicapped, and he's big. He can look menacing or friendly. He likes loud music and jigsaw puzzles and he's a loner. He's not violent, but sometimes he gets agitated and bites other residents.

Tell him to do something, his case file says, and he'll obey.

When three group home attendants rushed into Greene's house and ordered Kubicki to leave, he didn't put up a fight. He was, Greene says, "redirected" outside without a struggle.

Greene said she didn't realize Kubicki lived in the group home until the attendants led him across the street.

Greene made a police report that day and a warrant was issued later. Charged with illegal entry, a misdemeanor, Kubicki was arraigned and ordered to undergo testing to see if he should stand trial. Kubicki's mother, Judy Kubicki, said he had no idea of what was going on.

Kubicki has wound up in the middle of a long-simmering feud between the group home operators and the residents of the Stoney Cove neighborhood. And whether or not Kubicki understands what's going on, he's the one in the stew.

When Stoney Cove residents learned of plans for the group home, they circulated petitions to keep it out — Greene says she signed — and they even got an attorney to try to stop the deal on a technicality. It didn't work, and the home opened in May 1988.

Within two months, neighbors started complaining. The list of complaints grew. Some seem petty — like the time a blind resident accidentally stood in front of an open window with his pants down. Others have merit — like the complaints about a resident's wandering onto a neighbor's property or rummaging through the trash.

The group home had problems, there's no denying it. The state agency that supervises the home put it on a provisional license — meaning that the administrator could lose the contract to run it. After the Kubicki incident, a new administrator was brought in.

Gerald Provencal, director of Macomb-Oakland Regional Center (MORC), which supervises about 180 group homes in the area, accused the Stoney Cove residents and the city of Troy of being opposed to group homes. One Troy group home was burned down before it could open, one was shot up the day it opened, one got a bomb threat and another was purchased by neighbors to keep it from opening, Provencal said. Most group homes work out fine, he said.

When they don't work, people like Mark Kubicki wind up being victims, and group homes, which are a million times better than institutions, get a black eye.

Kubicki's mother said she worked for two years to get him into the Stoney Cove home because it was close to her house. When the move occurred this April, "it seemed almost too good to be true," she said.

It was.

Her son is now charged with a crime because the people who were supposed to watch him slipped up. And if that's not bad enough, MORC is moving him into a new group home, some 20 miles from his folks' home, to avoid any more problems in the neighborhood.

Mark Kubicki doesn't understand it. Is there any wonder why?

September 18, 1989

■

Cruel experiments leave many lessons

QUICK. ASK SOMEONE WHO JAMES STANLEY IS.

If you're lucky, you'll come across a dozen people who know that Stanley was among 1,000 soldiers tricked into taking powerful doses of LSD in the 1950s as part of a secret Army experiment on hallucinogenic drugs.

Stanley is seeking compensation from the government, so his name has been in the news.

But if you wait six months after the issue is settled and then ask the same question, you'll probably find only one or two people who vaguely remember that Stanley had something to do with secret drug testing.

Wait a couple of years, and only a few people with a special interest in the case will remember the abuse the government heaped upon James Stanley. Wait five years, and the facts about the experiment itself will become hazy. Ten years, and the haze will form into a question mark dotted with doubt: "That really didn't happen, did it?" Seventeen years, and the entire episode will be mostly forgotten. Gone. Wiped from the record of history we carry around with us every day.

Maybe in Stanley's case, it will take longer than 17 years to forget. Maybe the fact that soldiers, the defenders of our freedom, were used as human guinea pigs will keep this national scar tender to the touch of memory and morality.

I hope so. We need to remember the atrocities visited upon those soldiers, just as we need to remember the atrocities visited upon another group of men in something called the Tuskegee Study.

Quick. Ask someone what the Tuskegee Study was.

From 1932 to 1972, a total of 431 black men from Macon County, Ala., were denied treatment for syphilis so that government doctors could determine, through eventual autopsies, the long-term effects of the disease. Most of the men weren't told they had syphilis, so they passed it on — not only to their sexual partners, but to their children.

At least 28 black men, and maybe as many as 100, died as a direct result of untreated syphilis, because the U.S. Public Health Service had decided to conduct the human experiment.

Dozens of men went blind, lost their hearing or suffered damage to their nervous and circulatory systems.

The study started in 1932 when treatment for syphilis was long and hazardous but readily available. Fourteen years into the study, Public Health Service researchers wrote in an interim report:

"It is clear that, in the absence of treatment, the person infected with syphilis, even though he may escape the late crippling manifestations which lead directly to death, still runs a considerable risk of having his life span shortened by other fatal conditions. In addition, he can expect to experience more manifestations of ill health of all kinds than do uninfected persons."

That report was dated 1946, the same year that penicillin was discovered as a safe, effective cure for syphilis. Still, the experiment continued for another 26 years.

Men, black men, human beings, were allowed by the government to die so that doctors could cut them open on an autopsy table and study the effects of the disease.

The experiment ended shortly after it was made public. The remaining participants were given lifetime free medical care, as were some spouses and children. A successful class-action lawsuit resulted in monetary settlements for each participant.

As of July, 33 former participants were still alive, along with 39 wives or widows and 18 children who had contracted syphilis.

Yet, if you ask people about the Tuskegee Study, most will give you a blank look. If you give the word "syphilis" as a hint, some folks will get ready to fight. Some people have forgotten the experiment; some never knew it existed.

"People want to forget about it," said a government official who keeps track of the Tuskegee survivors.

But, whether it's syphilis or LSD, our reluctance to remember is almost as much a tragedy as the study itself.

September 25, 1989

■

City and nation are two-faced on race

QUIET AS IT'S KEPT, FOLKS ALL OVER TOWN HAVE BEEN TALKING for months about the possibility that Maryann Mahaffey could become City Council president and thus be a heartbeat away from the mayor's seat.

Several council candidates have been whispering about what could happen if Mahaffey, a white woman, gets the top council spot.

Now, the Rev. Jim Holley of Little Rock Baptist Church is in hot water because he made the whispers public.

In recent interviews he said Mahaffey's selection as council president would be the first sign of blacks' losing their power base in the city.

"It's not that she's bad or unkind," he said. "It's just that we waited and worked so long to get where we are." Councilman Clyde Cleveland said pretty much the same thing.

As expected, all hell broke loose; the fury focused on Holley. Ministers, pols and civil rights activists have taken him to task, calling his remarks racist and divisive.

The winds of moral outrage are swirling like Hurricane Hugo. Every truism you ever heard about race, equality and fairness is getting a new airing by critics.

As for Jim Holley, his eyes welled with tears as he tried to explain what he really meant. He said he had nothing against Mahaffey. He voted for her in the primary, and she's a fine, caring woman.

Well, you know what I think is wrong with Jim Holley? I think he has diarrhea of the mouth.

What he said about Mahaffey was just plain stupid.

But, like it or not, Holley's statements also reflect more truth about America than most folks care to admit. America and Americans are basically two-faced when it comes to race. We say one thing; we do something else.

It's the damnedest situation. On the one hand, we as a nation uphold and revere these incredibly complicated and liberating statements about freedom and equality for all human beings.

But when it comes to acting on our principles, it's a different story. We don't trust each other much. By and large, we don't live together, we don't send our children to the same schools, and we don't worship together.

Black folks, white folks, red, brown and yellow folks still measure and are measured by the color of their skin.

Sure, there are intentionally integrated neighborhoods. Mahaffey lives in one, as does Holley. There are churches and schools that are integrated. But that ain't the rule, and don't let anybody tell you otherwise.

Philosopher and historian W.E.B. Du Bois said more than 80 years ago that color is the key problem of this century. He was right. Race subtly and not so subtly affects almost every action we take. That's not new. Our Constitution suffers from the same racial and sexual schizophrenia that affects us today.

When the founding fathers talked about "we, the people," they weren't talking about the men in my family. They weren't talking about Maryann Mahaffey. They weren't talking about me. They were talking about free white men.

Remember. The Constitution had to be amended to give legal freedom to blacks and women.

We as a nation have labored under this crippling duality since Day One. Black folks in particular — but probably other folks, too — constantly do a balancing act between lofty principles we believe in and the harsh reality we live under.

So it is not surprising to me that some folks would start an ugly whisper campaign against Mahaffey. Our gains are fragile; our fears too often have become reality; our mistrust runs deep.

What does surprise me is that Holley would turn up — even inadvertently — the volume. While there's nothing wrong with wanting to have a black mayor, there's everything wrong with trying to keep someone from being elected to a certain position just because she is white.

What has happened to Mahaffey is ugly and unfair.

But don't be deceived. It is also as American as apple pie.

Mahaffey came in first in the race and became City Council president.

T-shirts provide cultural litmus test

I THOUGHT IT WAS JUST A $13 T-SHIRT. LONG-SLEEVED. BLACK. accented with a huge green, yellow and red design on the front.

I bought it about two weeks ago when my husband and I were in Washington, D.C., for a football game at the school our kid attends.

Actually, I bought two T-shirts. One for me, one for my husband. I also bought a bag of fresh-roasted peanuts and a book about slavery.

Those were just a few of the goods hawked by dozens of vendors who flanked both sides of the line leading to the stadium. I felt like I was running a gauntlet, but the line was so slow I could take baby steps.

And, instead of brandishing weapons, the vendors waved T-shirts, jewelry, political posters, books, peanuts, hot sausages and cold drinks.

I bought the book because I wanted something to help pass the time between the pregame activities and the halftime show. I bought the peanuts because no one was selling popcorn. As for the T-shirts, I bought them because they captured the spirit of the place.

Howard University was playing its homecoming game against More-house College. Both schools boast a rich history of educating generations of African-American students. Their distinction in the classroom does not spill onto the football field.

Still, that weekend gave me an ideal excuse to reach out and touch the person behind the voice that calls home collect to ask for money.

It had been almost three months since I stood in our front yard and waved good-bye as the Seeker of Wisdom and Truth headed off to school. I just wanted to make sure I'd know which kid to yell at if he brought someone home with him one weekend.

And it's a good thing my husband and I made that trip. The person I sent off to college in August had close-cropped hair and clean-shaven face.

The person who hugged me in front of my son's dorm had a full beard and a 2-inch shock of hair on the top of his head. He called me mom.

The Seeker is letting his hair grow so he can wear it in dreadlocks — thick ropes of hair that, I am told, were first popularized in ancient Egypt. I shouldn't have been surprised.

This is the same person who turned up last year with the outline of the continent of Africa shaved into the hair on one side of his head and the profile of Queen Nefertiti on the other.

It's his way of letting people know that he glories in his African heritage. It's also a surefire way to get us to do a double take.

To him, his hair is a cultural litmus test: If you understand it, it eventually will bring a smile of recognition to your face. If you don't understand it, it'll make you squirm — or worse.

Darned if the same thing didn't happen when my husband and I wore those T-shirts from the homecoming game.

On the front is a huge drawing of the continent of Africa, colored in bold swatches of red, yellow and green. The words "International Homegirls (or Homeboys) Club" are inscribed in bold letters across the middle of the continent.

The rest of the space is filled with the names of dozens of cities around the world, from Detroit to Nairobi and from Paris to Soweto.

The T-shirt represents the dispersion of African people around the world and the common ancestry that unites the children of Africa, no matter where they are.

When I wore the T-shirt in public, it took folks a few seconds to process the words.

Then the reactions set in. Some folks, most of them the children of Africa, smiled or nodded in recognition. Others, both black and white, averted their eyes.

They seemed puzzled, but afraid to ask questions, lest they get trapped in a conversation about that "Africa stuff." A small number of individuals hardened their faces against the exaltation of ancestry.

Like my kid's hair, that shirt also turned out to be a cultural litmus test. And a whole lot of folks didn't pass it.

5

POLITICS

On the front: *Entertainer Stevie Wonder and Detroit Mayor Coleman Young.*

■

Who's pulling
those strings?

I WAS TOO CHICKEN TO ADMIT IT BEFORE, BUT AFTER RECENT events, I feel much more comfortable saying it.

Ronald Reagan and Howdy Doody look like identical twins.

Honest. I'm serious.

If I didn't know better, I'd swear they were separated at birth when a lonely wood-carver named Gepetto kidnapped Howdy's twin brother, Rowdy, now known as Ronnie, from the leafy boughs of their mother, a giant elm. Gepetto, who earlier had mixed success with another little wooden boy named Pinocchio, nicknamed the little sapling Dutch as a tribute to his roots.

For years I have been struck by the remarkable physical resemblance between the 40th president of the United States and that delightful, freckle-faced marionette who thrilled a generation of youngsters in the early days of television.

Think about it.

Both have broad faces, apple cheeks, patent-leather hair, wide smiles, jug ears and twinkling eyes filled with wonder. Both are cowboys at heart who move with wooden grace.

Remember how good old Howdy used to bounce around the stage at Doodyville, head bobbing and arms all ajingle? Geez, he was cute.

Now, picture the president as he stands in the doorway of Air Force One and snaps off a salute for the cameras. Golly, he's even more photogenic than Howdy.

Admit it. The guys are twins, endearing little buckaroos who march and talk to the music of a maestro who pulls the strings and puts words in their mouths.

Even though they were separated at birth, they branched out in the same direction.

I always thought Howdy had a crush on Princess Summer-Fall-Winter-Spring, a gentle beauty who, unlike the puppet star of the show, could walk and talk and sing all by herself.

Rowdy fell in love with Nancy, another gentle princess who wears ball gowns instead of buckskin and often is seen whispering dialogue into Rowdy's ear.

Howdy doesn't have a mean bone in his body or an evil thought — or any other kind for that matter — rattling in his head.

As for Rowdy, the resemblance is more than skin deep.

Howdy couldn't have made it without Buffalo Bob, his old buddy who was always looking over his shoulder and keeping him out of harm's way.

Rowdy relied on a crew of friends from California who steered him through, and sometimes into, troubled waters.

Howdy never knew what time it was. Why else do you think every show started with the announcer's asking, "Say, kids, what time is it?" Howdy wouldn't know if he was in a box or a bathtub unless somebody told him.

Rowdy gets a little confused about details, too. Remember when he joked about bombing Russia — into a live microphone?

Then there are the times he dozes off during cabinet meetings because he looks at the clock and gets the big hand and the little hand mixed up.

The similarities go on and on, but I don't have to bore you with any more facts.

Larry Speakes, the former White House spokesman, proved my point.

In his memoirs, "Speaking Out," Speakes revealed that he had whipped up nifty quotes and attributed them to the president without the president's approval.

But there's one important difference between Howdy and Rowdy. With Howdy, you could see the wires controlling his every move.

With Rowdy, it's harder to tell who's pulling the strings.

September 16, 1988

■

Fetus should not be ward of court

IT'S A GOOD THING FOR JUDGE VALDEMAR WASHINGTON THAT I can't work miracles. If I could, I'd strike him pregnant.

That's right, I'd bless the Genesee County circuit judge with a womb and other appropriate parts, pop a 10-week-old fetus in his belly and give him a 24-hour-a-day case of morning sickness.

Washington is the jurist who ordered a Flint woman in her 10th week of pregnancy not to have an abortion. The woman, Shawn Lewis, filed for divorce in January from her husband, Carlton. While the divorce was pending, Shawn Lewis got pregnant. She decided to have an abortion and told her estranged husband about her plans. The husband didn't agree. He said he had certain rights to the unborn child, and he went before Washington to try to block the abortion.

The judge legally enjoined the wife from getting an abortion. Washington said he found conflicts between Michigan's divorce laws and

160

the U.S. Supreme Court ruling on abortion. The judge ruled, in essence, that, in divorce cases, the court has jurisdiction over the fetus.

A state appeals court panel overruled Washington and voided the injunction against the abortion. Then the state Supreme Court agreed to settle the case, but reinstated the abortion ban pending the court's decision.

Through all of this, Shawn Lewis has been forced to carry a fetus she doesn't want and to abide by the wishes of the husband she wants to dump.

What's happening here stinks. The U.S. Supreme Court has ruled that a woman does not have to get permission from her husband to have an abortion. Legal opponents of the judge's decision also cite a 1976 U.S. Supreme Court ruling that said, "Since it is the woman who physically bears the child and who is the more directly and immediately affected by the pregnancy . . . the balance weighs in her favor."

That makes sense to me. What didn't make sense, though, was why Shawn Lewis didn't simply take what seemed to be two obvious solutions to her problem:

I wondered why she didn't just drop the divorce suit, get the abortion, and then start the divorce suit all over again from scratch. An even quicker method, I thought, would have been to go to a doctor and get an abortion.

Under the second plan, the worst thing she would face would be a contempt of court citation and a fine — a $250 fine and 30 days in jail. Contempt seemed the lesser evil.

Well, I was wrong on both counts. And I was wrong because I, like a lot of people, I think, was so blinded by the glare over the abortion issue that I lost sight of individuals.

The Lewises have a 16-month-old child, and both parents have said they want custody.

Shawn Lewis is afraid to get an abortion because she fears she would then lose the 16-month-old. A lawyer told me that judges do not look kindly on people who ignore their orders. The divorce judge, in this case Judge Washington, could take her deliberate violation of his order into consideration as he figured out custody of the toddler.

As for dropping the suit, it's not that simple. At this stage of the proceedings, Shawn Lewis would have to get permission from Washington to drop the case. And there's a possibility that Carlton Lewis could object and his objections could be taken into account.

So, Shawn Lewis is stuck. If she goes ahead with the abortion, she could lose custody of her toddler. If she tries to drop the case, she probably would have to deal with the judge who set her on this tortured path and a husband who wants the unborn child.

But there's still another problem.

If by some wild stretch of the law this woman is forced to bear a child

161

she has said she does not want, just think of the effect that would have on that child. The youngster would learn that Mother wanted to abort him or her, and the child could read all about it in old newspapers.

Surely, the state Supreme Court will act swiftly and wisely to right this dreadful situation.

If that doesn't happen, I'm hoping for a medical miracle for Judge Washington — and the daddy, too.

The case went to the U.S. Supreme Court, which quickly dissolved the injunction. Shawn Lewis had the abortion.

October 3, 1986

■

Hot talk raises heat when it's your home

OH MY, HE'S DONE IT AGAIN.

Mayor Coleman Young, the Peck's Bad Boy of urban politics, has shot off his mouth again on the taboo subjects of race and guns and crime.

During an interview on a Canadian television station, Young said he had no problem with gun control as long as all Americans gave up their guns.

But, he continued, "I'll be damned if I'm going to let them collect guns in the City of Detroit while we're surrounded by hostile suburbs and the whole rest of the state who have guns, and where you have vigilantes practicing Ku Klux Klan in the wilderness with automatic weapons."

Now, what hizzoner said wasn't new. It was a variation on an old theme.

He's been saying for years that Detroiters have to be armed against bad guys. In September, before the Canadian interview, he had said it would be a disaster to ask citizens to disarm themselves, in view of the rampant crime in the city.

On No Crime Day, which came just one day after that Canadian TV interview, the mayor repeated his feelings:

"I'm not prepared to disarm the people of Detroit while everybody else in the nation and world has arms, while the Ku Klux Klan and vigilante outfits are training in the wilderness, some of them openly, for the next race war."

Most folks didn't go crazy over the mayor's other statements. But the hostile suburbs line exploded like a bomb. I wonder why the difference?

Surely, part of the reason is that those of us who live and work in the area are accustomed to the mayor's blunt responses.

162

Mayor Young doesn't mince any words. He'll charm the socks off you and then hold your bare feet to the fire of his rhetoric.

Still, rhetoric doesn't explain the rage over his radio comments.

Oakland County Prosecutor L. Brooks Patterson, who also shoots from the lip, called a news conference to say that Detroiters are responsible for much of the crime in Southfield.

Patterson said he was tired of Young bashing the suburbs. The suburbs, Patterson said, "are being victimized by marauding gangs from Detroit."

My, my, my. Coleman is so bad. He should be more positive, more diplomatic, more statesmanlike. Lots of folks criticized him for talking about hostile suburbs.

Well, buffalo chips.

No one went bonkers about this gun control issue until Young hit on the suburbs. Be honest. Some folks in the suburbs are hostile toward Detroiters. Some Detroiters are hostile toward suburbanites. Some whites don't like blacks and some blacks don't like whites.

I think a lot of people who should know better just went out of control when the mayor brought the issue of racism right to our doorstep, our mutual borders. He can talk about criminals in Detroit (translate that black-on-black crime) and most folks in the suburbs don't get upset. He can talk about the crazy, wild-eyed white supremacists out West, and most folks don't get hot under the collar.

But bring the issue down to Eight Mile Road — bring it home — and tempers flare.

Sure Coleman didn't need to spout off the way he did. His comments merely provided fodder for his enemies. But let's not fight about hostile suburbs right now.

How much better it would be if the mayor spent more time and energy taking a vocal lead in the fight against the violence that is claiming our children. How much better it would be if my mayor used his incredible charisma to spur citizens to change those institutions that contribute to the problem of juvenile violence.

How much better it would be if Coleman Young would light the way for me and my child and my neighbor in Detroit. Then I'll worry about the hostile suburbs.

January 27, 1989

■

Cook's advice
has meaning for trial

YEARS AGO WHEN I WAS A CAMP COUNSELOR, I USED TO SPEND MY

free hours sitting in the kitchen and soaking up wisdom from the camp cook. Her name was Mrs. Penson, and she had the kind of street wisdom — or walking-around sense, as she would call it — that comes wrapped in experience, not sheepskin.

Mrs. Penson spent as much time urging the counselors — college students mainly — to excel as she did stirring pots and baking chicken.

No matter what you decided to do in life, she used to say, do it well. If you're going to a teacher, be a good teacher; if you're going to be a bum, be a good bum.

Don't sell yourself short in life.

Well, Mrs. Penson's steamy wisdom has popped into my head as I follow the trial of 36th District Judge Leon Jenkins, charged with taking $3,000 in cash, jewelry valued at $500, a gun and groceries, among other things, to fix traffic tickets and other misdemeanor violations.

The trial has been hard to miss. Nightly news shows have carried segments purporting to show Jenkins asking for gifts in return for favors.

Using secret cameras and hidden microphones, federal investigators taped and recorded what they claim are scenes showing Jenkins asking Detroit grocer Sabah Dickow for $100, a pound of ham, a free lunch at Joe Muer's or a gun. Dickow was working with the feds as an undercover snitch and was using $100,000 in federal money to finance his taped generosity.

Jenkins' attorney, Cornelius Pitts, said the case against his client is racially motivated. And, tapes aside, there may indeed be more than a grain of truth to that argument. This country is shot through with racism. I'm not saying the charges are bogus; I'm just saying that racism lives.

In any event, Pitts said Dickow darned near forced money on Jenkins who was lonely and gullible because of the recent death of his wife.

If Jenkins was guilty of anything, Pitts said early in the trial, it was of being naive.

"Indeed, he may be gullible, this man may indeed be crude, this man may indeed be stupid, he may be arrogant in a variety of things, but he's no crook," Pitts argued.

"When money is mentioned by the judge, it was as a loan," Pitts said.

Well, the trial is a long way from being finished. Jenkins hasn't been found guilty of anything, except — if you believe his attorney — stupidity.

And stupidity isn't a criminal offense. If it were, a whole lot of people I know would be wearing jail stripes instead of three-piece suits.

But I have to admit this. The penny-ante nature of the alleged bribes/gifts/loans boggles the mind. Judges in the 36th District Court are paid $88,000 a year — that's darned near $3,500 every two weeks before taxes.

While the government tapes produced at the trail may not wind up supporting the criminal charges, they certainly show that Jenkins got in

164

trouble over what we call chump change.

In the tapes, for example, Jenkins asks Dickow for a free lunch at Carl's Chop House or Joe Muer's restaurant. "Why don't you take me and my lady out to lunch tomorrow?" Jenkins asks in a taped conversation from January 1985.

Another tape has Jenkins taking what Dickow claimed was $100.

Then there's a tape allegedly showing Jenkins taking a box of bullets from Dickow and then asking for a gun.

Honest. Is there anybody out there who didn't cringe when he or she heard about those tapes and heard the paltry amounts mentioned?

Jenkins: I want you to give me the stuff so I, I can deal with it. Yeah, what's happening, you got any money, man?

Dickow: Yeah. I got money.

Jenkins: I need some money, man.

Dickow: What kind money you want?

Jenkins: I need about a hundred bucks.

Dickow: You got it.

No matter what the outcome of the trial, I can't help but wish that Judge Jenkins had spent a little time in Mrs. Penson's kitchen.

Jenkins was acquitted on four counts of extortion. The jury was unable to reach a verdict on a racketeering charge. He is appealing a decision by the prosecution to retry him on the racketeering charge.

March 24, 1989

■

Justice is blind, but not to a raise

RECENTLY, CHIEF JUSTICE WILLIAM REHNQUIST, IN A HIGHLY unusual move, held a news conference to ask for a little favor.

Rehnquist asked Congress — which turned down a 51 percent pay hike for lawmakers, federal judges and high-ranking government officials — to give federal judges a 30 percent raise so the judges could afford to send their kids to college.

All Rehnquist wants is a little compassion and understanding.

Well, when attorney Arthur Greenstone read about Rehnquist's plea, Greenstone hit the ceiling — actually, the fax machine and the mailbox.

Within days, the Birmingham lawyer had blazed a trail of outrage from Detroit to the Washington office of the chief justice, with a few pols thrown in for good measure.

About a month before Rehnquist requested those pay hikes — which would jack up a federal judge's salary $27,000 to $35,000 a year — Rehnquist wrote the majority opinion in the "Poor Joshua" case.

Nine-year-old Joshua DeShaney of Wisconsin was so severely beaten by his father that the boy suffered permanent brain damage when he was four years old. He is paralyzed and will spend the rest of his life in an institution for the profoundly retarded.

But Joshua's mistreatment wasn't some darkly held secret. For 14 months, from January 1983 to March 1984, a Winnebago County Department of Social Services caseworker visited the boy's home some 20 times, saw a number of suspicious injuries on his head and received reports of suspected abuse from hospital emergency rooms where Joshua had been treated.

The caseworker did essentially nothing, except to record those incidents carefully in her files and note her suspicions that someone was physically abusing the child.

After Joshua received emergency-room care for suspected abuse in November 1983, the caseworker twice visited his home but was told he was too ill to see her. Even then, no action was taken.

In March 1984, Joshua was beaten so severely that he fell into a coma and required emergency brain surgery. The child's brain showed effects of years of beatings. Joshua's father was convicted of child abuse and served two years in prison.

Joshua's parents were divorced when he was an infant and the father had custody. The mother lived in Wyoming and learned of the abuse only after the near-fatal beating.

Joshua and his mother sued the county, charging that its failure to act, despite repeated instances of abuse, had deprived Joshua of certain constitutional rights.

Finally, the U.S. Supreme Court upheld lower court decisions and ruled, six to three, that state officials had no constitutional obligation to protect Joshua from his dad.

In an impassioned dissent, Justice Harry Blackmun wrote: "Today, the Court purports to be the dispassionate oracle of the law, unmoved by 'natural sympathy.' ... Faced with the choice, I would adopt a 'sympathetic' reading ... which recognizes that compassion need not be exiled from the province of judging."

It was also Blackmun who wrote: "Poor Joshua! Victim of repeated attacks by an irresponsible, bullying, cowardly and intemperate father and abandoned by (state officials) ... who did essentially nothing. ... It is a sad commentary upon American life and constitutional principles."

But Rehnquist, speaking for the majority, wrote: "Judges and lawyers, like other humans, are moved by natural sympathy in a case like this to find a way for Joshua and his mother to receive adequate compensation for the grievous harm inflicted upon them. But, before yielding to that impulse, it is well to remember once again that the harm was inflicted not by the State of Wisconsin, but by Joshua's father."

And what does this have to do with Rehnquist's plea for money?

Well, to paraphrase Arthur Greenstone: He who cannot show compassion for someone else has a hell of a lot of nerve asking some for himself.

The federal judges got their pay raise.

June 16, 1989

■

Claims in probe
swirl beyond logic

THE WORD FOR TODAY, BOYS AND GIRLS, IS DUMB. THAT'S RIGHT, dumb, as in stupid, dull, dense, doltish, asinine, lamebrained and inept.

And this morning we're going to examine the many wonderful ways that this word can be applied to the charges and denials, countercharges and counter-denials surrounding the supposed police probe into the sex life of Mayor Coleman Young's former girlfriend.

But first, a little background.

All . . . ahem . . . heck broke out when unnamed Detroit police sources and an identified Water and Sewerage Department employee charged that a top-secret police unit had snooped into the sex life of a woman who had filed a paternity suit against Young.

According to reports, the peeping cops were trying to gather information about whether former City of Detroit official Annivory Calvert knew, in the biblical sense, other men at the same time she dated the mayor.

Such information could have been useful in court if blood tests in the paternity suit had proved inconclusive. As it was, the blood tests showed that Young is the papa.

Well, the next thing you know, Young is swearing — literally — that he didn't know anything about any such probe. The city employee who talked on the record to reporters was moved abruptly to a less desirable job. He called it a demotion; his bosses called it a transfer.

Then the sewage really started to hit the fan. City Council President Erma Henderson, who is running for mayor, called for an investigation. Henderson also said she thought her home and office phones were bugged by the Detroit police. You know, that reminds me, boys and girls. A few years back, Henderson said in an open council session that she had heard a rumor that a fast-food company might be operated by the Ku Klux Klan to destroy blacks.

Anyway, Calvert, who now works in California, filed a complaint with the Wayne County Prosecutor's Office when she learned of the alleged snooping. The prosecutor is going to review the case.

If Calvert's name rings a bell, it could be because a Detroit cop said she once claimed diplomatic immunity when the cop told her to move her car. She denied it.

But back to this story. Mayor Young swings back by announcing that the police department will investigate the charges. The police chief heaps so much praise on the snoop troop that you'd think they were candidates for sainthood.

At least, you might have thought that until the department announced that Calvert and her sister had been under investigation for making a false stolen car claim to their auto insurance company. The head of the snoop troop said he learned of the alleged scam in March. The informant? The same Water and Sewerage employee who told reporters about the sex probe. The head snoop staunchly denied he ever asked the informant about Calvert's personal or social life.

As the situation now stands, everyone is calling everyone else a liar.

I don't know if we'll ever get to the truth of this tangled affair. But I do know this: If you want to believe any of the stories about police snooping and car insurance scams, you also have to believe that the key folks in this mess are just plain dumb.

Annivory Calvert, who gave reporters the name of the demoted city employee, would have to be dumber than dirt to call for an investigation if she, indeed, was part of an insurance scam.

The demoted city employee would have to be dumber than sludge to rat on the police unit that he supposedly told about the car scam.

The snoop troop would have to dumber than sewage to concoct a story about a car scam to cover up its involvement in sex snooping.

And finally, those who believe the mayor had to know something about the snoop troop's alleged prying also have to believe that Coleman A. Young is the dumbest son of a politician to come out of the West since . . . well, since Richard Nixon tried to stonewall Watergate.

October 2, 1989

■

Eberhard should
learn to take a bus

POOR BABY.

Detroit City Councilman David Eberhard had a public temper tantrum because he's had a run of bad luck with his city-owned cars.

In fact, I hear he was so angry he stormed out of a council session vowing to rent a car and charge it to the city.

So, there!

Eberhard's car troubles started about a month ago. He was making a U-turn on East Jefferson when, he said, his brakes gave out and he was hit by a motorcyclist whom he had cut off.

Eberhard suffered facial cuts and a broken nose; police said the motorcyclist appeared to have an injured ankle. Eberhard didn't see the motorcycle because, as he explained at the time: "It was in my blind spot."

In case you didn't know, elected city officials — and some appointed ones — get a city-owned car. Most folks don't give it a second thought until someone lucky enough to have a city car starts complaining about it.

Well, Eberhard started complaining at this council session. According to a Free Press account of that meeting, Eberhard was steaming because the previous night the fourth city car lent to him since the Aug. 24 accident had conked out on St. Jean near Warren. Eberhard said the other three loaners had brake, horn and rear-wheel problems.

The episodes obviously left the dear man at his wit's end.

"We're being treated like second-class citizens!" he yelled at his colleagues Thursday morning. "What do I have to do, get killed, then you can pass a memorial resolution?"

Then he stalked out of the session.

Well, no one wants Eberhard — or anyone else — to get hurt again in one of those naughty, naughty, naughty city cars. So, being a good citizen and being concerned about Eberhard's well-being, I set out one morning to learn what ordinary people do when their cars conk out.

I wanted to lift the veil of secrecy that prevents Eberhard from knowing how to solve this nettlesome problem. I hit the bus stops.

"Pardon me, madam," I said to a 71-year-old woman who was sitting on a bench on Woodward near the old Hudson's downtown store. "What do you do when your car doesn't work?"

"I don't have a car," she said. "I ride the bus."

The woman, who was a kitchen helper in Detroit public schools before retiring, rides the bus to Wayne State University, where she's finishing a degree in sociology. When she gets it, she plans to open a preschool program.

I tried again.

"Pardon me, sir," I said to a 62-year-old retired factory worker standing on Woodward. "How do you get around when your car doesn't work?"

"I ride the bus," he said. The gentleman said he hasn't driven since he had a stroke some seven years ago. But, he added, when he had a car and it broke down, he just took the bus.

I moved on.

"Pardon me, sir," I said to a 20-year-old waiter standing near Michigan and Shelby. "If you have a car, how do you get around when it's broken?"

"I catch the bus," he said. In fact, he catches two buses in the morning and two in the evening. It's a 90-minute ride each way. One day when he gets enough money, maybe he'll buy a car. I reckon if he ever gets elected to the council, he could store his privately owned car and tool around in a city one.

I pressed on.

"Pardon me, madam," I said to a 65-year-old woman who was heading across town to do some errands. "How do you get around when your car doesn't work?"

"I don't have a car," she said. "I had one last winter, but it broke down on me. Now I take the bus all the time."

I could have talked to lots more people, but I had enough information to fashion a reply to Eberhard's "what do I have to do. ... "

The answer: Catch The Bus.

After all, 215,000 riders — many of them taxpayers who cough up the money for Eberhard's car and $57,770-a-year salary — do it every day.

November 1, 1989

■

Matter of principle
hinders drug fight

PRESIDENT GEORGE BUSH HAS VETOED THE DISTRICT OF Columbia's 1990 budget, which would have allowed the city to expand the use of federal and local tax dollars to finance abortions for poor women.

Now, in case you've forgotten your history, the district must have federal government approval of its budget whether the money comes from local sources — which provide 86 percent of the budget — or federal subsidies.

The budget in question would have allowed the district to use federal funds for abortions in cases of rape, incest and threats to a pregnant woman's life, and local funds to pay for abortions for the poor on demand.

Pundits viewed the president's veto as his way of delivering on his pledge to oppose abortion except when the life of a pregnant woman is at risk.

Well, now, I'm all for politicians keeping their word. And I can understand why Mr. Bush, being a decent man, would be loath to break his word to his antiabortion supporters.

But there's just this one tiny thing I don't understand about the moral posture the president has assumed on this issue. What the hell happened to all of his concern about Dooney?

Dooney is the little boy Bush mentioned at the end of his nationally televised Sept. 6 speech on drugs. According to the president, Dooney had, until shortly before the speech, lived in a crack house in a suburb of Washington, D.C.

"In Dooney's neighborhood, children don't flinch at the sound of gunfire. And when they play, they pretend to sell each other small white rocks they call crack," the president said.

"Life at home was so cruel that Dooney begged his teachers to let him sleep on the floor at school. And, when asked about his future, the 6-year-old Dooney answered: 'I don't want to sell drugs, but I will probably have to.'"

The nation surely winced at the thought of that poor little baby curled up on the floor, trying to get enough rest so he could survive another night in the crack house.

Then the president said with reassuring authority: "Well, Dooney does not have to sell drugs. No child in America should have to live like this. Together, as a people, we can save these kids. . . . But the war on drugs will be hard-won, neighborhood by neighborhood, block by block, child by child."

And what does the president's stand on abortion have to do with little Dooney?

Bush's veto also knocked out $32 million in extra money the district had planned to use to launch a stepped-up war on drugs. As you surely know by now, the District of Columbia has surpassed Detroit as the nation's latest crime and crack hot spot.

Drugs are rampant in D.C. Crime is soaring and young people are dying in the streets.

The district's budget would have allowed the city to help hire about 700 additional police officers and eight associate judges. In addition, the budget would have increased jail space, established on-demand drug treatment for pregnant women and set up special after-school programs for youngsters.

That $32 million wouldn't have been a magic cure to Washington's problems. It would, however, have given a heck of a jump start to another of the president's pledges: namely to make the nation's capital a model in the fight against illegal drugs.

Bush said he was compelled to veto the budget because he opposes the use of federal funds for abortions except when a pregnant woman's life is

171

at stake.

But what about little Dooney's life? That's what I want to know. It doesn't matter that he doesn't live in the district. Bush used the heart-wrenching image of that little boy to represent all the innocent children who suffer from the illegal drug trade.

Then, with his budget veto, the president turned his back on all the little Dooneys in Washington, D.C. The president chose a fetus, an unborn child, over a 6-year-old boy whom he had used to make a good point in his speech.

Bush and his supporters might label his veto as principled or even honorable.

As for me, I call it obscene.

November 10, 1989

■

Young relishes
a hearty last laugh

SEE MAYOR YOUNG.
See Mayor Young laugh.
Laugh, Mayor Young, laugh.
Hee hee hee hee hee.

That infectious Coleman Young chuckle starts somewhere deep in his belly and works its way up to the throat. Then it puffs his jowls, crinkles those steely eyes and tickles its way past his mustache.

Mayor Young was laughing Tuesday . . . and Wednesday and Thursday and probably today. As he sees it, he not only defeated Tom Barrow; he beat the media.

For years, Young has been singing the "mean media blues." In chorus after chorus, he has accused the TV stations and the newspapers of being unfair and overly critical in our coverage of Detroit and the man who runs it.

This election year, Young spent more time attacking the media than attacking his opponent. Of course, Young virtually ignored challenger Tom Barrow, so it's safe to say the mayor spent more time combing his hair than attacking Barrow.

For the first time in a general election, the Free Press endorsed a challenger to Young. The Free Press and the Detroit News echoed, in one form or another, Barrow's "Time for a Change" slogan. Both urged Detroit citizens to vote down the stubborn, feisty and quick-tempered politician.

Detroit voters responded by re-electing Young to a record-setting fifth term.

See Mayor Young.

See Mayor Young run.

Run, Mayor Young, run.

Hee hee hee hee hee.

People in the street — and those in high office — never claimed Coleman Young is perfect. In fact, his audacity is part of his charm, part of the magic that welds him to the voters.

As the old folks say, "He don't take no stuff."

And to people who spend their days "taking stuff" from bosses, co-workers, shopkeepers, creditors, social workers and even kids, Coleman's outspokenness gives voice to their pent-up feelings.

Sure, Coleman is a hardheaded, quick-tempered, feisty old son of a so-and-so. But his supporters quickly remind you that he is "our" hardheaded, quick-tempered, feisty old son of a so-and-so.

The final tally in Tuesday's race did not give Young an overwhelming mandate. The mayor snared 56 percent of the vote, leaving him with the slimmest victory margin since his first bid for the mayor's seat in 1973.

Regardless of the width of the victory margin, the voters once again handed the old gray fox the key to the executive office. His opponents would probably say he was given the key to the chicken coop.

And as hizzoner would probably reply, "What do they know? They lost."

See Mayor Young.

See Mayor Young win.

Win, Mayor Young, win.

Hee hee hee hee hee.

Some people will never understand why Detroiters vote for Young despite problems during his administration.

He was woefully slow to act on the deadly combination of crime, drugs and kids. The cost overruns on Chrysler Corp.'s Jefferson project are astronomical. Young waited far too long to get serious about demolishing abandoned buildings.

He is stubborn and much too isolated from the streets. But his name is synonymous with Detroit.

Part of the reason for Young's repeated re-election stems from his remarkable reputation as an unflinching fighter for the poor and the oppressed, regardless of color. Another part comes from his flat-out refusal to give up on Detroit when others were trying to erect a tombstone in a town that still held a million people.

Young and Detroit — the mayor and the metropolis — are tough, street-savvy survivors. Scarred and a little sore from too many fights, they can still dazzle you with their finery and take your breath away with

173

their bold gambles on the future.

Four years from now, Detroiters may well be ready to send the old gray fox into retirement. But until then, if you're looking for the keys to the executive office, he's got 'em.

Hee hee hee hee hee.

July 1, 1988

■

A dream city — at your fingertips

SOMETIMES IT'S FUN TO IMAGINE WHAT WOULD HAPPEN IF THE seemingly impossible occurred.

Suppose Motown superstar Stevie Wonder not only ran for but also became the mayor of Detroit. It's not that outrageous a thought. Stevie Wonder already has said he might seek the job in the future.

I'd vote for him, no questions asked. Heck, I voted for Jesse and Walter and Jimmy, and I've pulled the lever for Coleman more times than I can remember. Voting for Stevie Wonder would be like opening the windows in a musty parlor and letting the sunshine in.

Plus, if you vote for Stevie, you could wind up with a cast of mayoral appointees that would increase citizen participation by 1,000 percent.

In the Wonder Cabinet, for example, the director of media relations would be Aretha Franklin. After all, who would dare give Detroit a bum rap after listening to Aretha explain the importance of "Respect"?

The other possible appointees:

Chief of police: Ray Charles, who would warn felons to "Hit the Road, Jack." Edwin Starr, going by the code name "Agent Double-O Soul," would handle the plainclothes detail.

The missing persons bureau would be headed by the Coasters, who have been "Searchin'" for 30 years.

Rumor control: If someone phoned to report "I heard it through the grapevine," Marvin Gaye (I know he's dead, but this is my fantasy) would have the Temptations convince the caller it's "Just My Imagination."

Consumer affairs: Smokey Robinson and the Miracles would urge consumers to "Shop Around" before making that final purchase.

Detroit Historical Museum: Martha and the Vandellas would throw open the door to anyone who wanted to "Come and Get These Memories."

Summer work program: Youngsters hanging out on the corner wouldn't escape the long shadow of the Silhouettes, who would tell them to "Get a Job."

Finance department: Barrett Strong would travel to Lansing and Washington with the city's plea for "Money, That's What I Want."

Jails: Sam Cooke would start a work program and put prisoners on the "Chain Gang."

Downtown development: Thelma Houston would keep businesses downtown by telling them, "Don't Leave Me This Way." The Jackson Five would give decision makers at Hudson's, Sears, Saks and Highland Superstores the following message: "I Want You Back."

Casino gaming: Johnny Mathis wouldn't necessarily tell you what your "Chances Are" of winning the jackpot, but he'd make sure you had a "Wonderful! Wonderful!" time.

Fire Department: Only a fool would dare play with matches after the Platters explain that "Smoke Gets in Your Eyes."

Animal control: Jackie Wilson would tell pet owners, "I'll Be Satisfied" when you stop your canine friends from "Doggin' Around."

The municipal garage sale in Cobo Hall: To prove that all items, even broken ones, have value, Patti LaBelle of the Blue Belles would reveal how much money she made when "I Sold My Heart to the Junkman."

Public Library: The Monotones would make the "Book of Love" the book of the month.

Friend of the Court: Parents who try to skip out on child support payments would be told by the Supremes to "Stop! In the Name of Love!"

Family planning: Nat King Cole would travel from school to school telling teenagers they are "Too Young to Go Steady." Nat would have the Midnighters relate the sad story of what happened after unwed "Annie Had a Baby."

Keeper of public morals: Gladys Knight and the Pips would put the Contours on a "Midnight Train to Georgia" because their "First I Look at the Purse" attitude has led so many city youths astray.

And that, with a lot of help from my friends, is how my Mayor Stevie would work his Wonders.